Praise for *Leading the Epic Revolution:
How CIOs Drive Innovation and
Create Value Across the Enterprise*

Modern markets are changing and evolving at an ever-increasing pace. Future success will require a culture that embraces continuous improvement and rapid innovation. The stories and advice in Hunter's new book will definitely help those who read it optimize and refine their innovation strategies.

—Hunter W. Jones, VP, Enterprise Services,
and CIO, Cameron International Corporation

Great stories, excellent advice, and timely, practical strategies as companies and executives manage through the transition to social, mobile, and cloud. This is a book worth reading from cover to cover.

—Tony Zingale, Chairman and CEO, Jive Software

Leading the Epic Revolution details the processes behind the innovation cultures at highly successful companies such as GE, IBM, AT&T, Box, Facebook, Netflix, and many others. I recommend this book for all forward-thinking executives.

—Mike Kail, VP, Information Technology, Netflix

LEADING
THE EPIC
REVOLUTION

LEADING

THE EPIC

REVOLUTION

How CIOs Drive Innovation and Create Value Across the Enterprise

HUNTER MULLER

WILEY

Published by John Wiley & Sons, Inc., Hoboken, New Jersey.
Published simultaneously in Canada.

For general information on our other products and services or for technical support, please contact our Customer Care Department within the United States at (800) 762-2974, outside the United States at (317) 572-3993 or fax (317) 572-4002.

Wiley publishes in a variety of print and electronic formats and by print-on-demand. Some material included with standard print versions of this book may not be included in e-books or in print-on-demand. If this book refers to media such as a CD or DVD that is not included in the version you purchased, you may download this material at http://booksupport.wiley.com. For more information about Wiley products, visit www.wiley.com.

Library of Congress Cataloging-in-Publication Data:

Muller, Hunter, 1960–
 Leading the epic revolution : how CIOs drive innovation and create value across the enterprise / Hunter Muller.
   pages cm. — (CIO series)
 Includes bibliographical references and index.
  ISBN 978-1-118-34047-9 (cloth); ISBN 978-1-118-43189-4 (ebk.);
ISBN 978-1-118-43193-1 (ebk.); ISBN 978-1-118-43194-8 (ebk.)
  1. Information technology—Management. 2. Technological innovations—Management. 3. Diffusion of innovations—Management. 4. Chief information officers. I. Title.
  HD30.2.M84947 2013
  658.4'038—dc23

                                                              2013002822

Printed in the United States of America

10 9 8 7 6 5 4 3 2 1

For Sandra, Brice, and Chase

CONTENTS

FOREWORD: INNOVATING FOR CONTINUAL GROWTH AND PROSPERITY

All companies have different needs and priorities. What all companies have in common, however, is the need to grow. And growth, to an investor, is best measured by increased value.

There are a relatively small number of ways to generate enduring value. Companies can introduce new products or services, attract new customers, and open new markets. They can also improve the quality of their existing products, raise their level of efficiency, and leverage economies of scale.

Accomplishing any of those objectives requires innovation. Companies cannot simply stand still and keep doing the same things they were doing yesterday. The world is changing continually, and companies have to keep pace or risk falling behind.

At McKesson, we fully understand that we live in changing times. We are not a consumer brand, but our presence is extraordinary. We are the largest pharmaceutical distributor in North America, distributing one-third of the medicines used every day.

We also develop and install health-care IT systems that eliminate the need for paper prescriptions and paper medical records. Our software and hardware are used in more than 70 percent of the nation's hospitals with more than 200 beds. Our hospital information system solutions include electronic health record system (EHR) and clinical decision support systems, 3-D radiology imaging systems, and analytics designed for health care. Our Healthcare IT division also serves diverse areas within the health industry by offering solutions such as pharmacy automation and medical claims management software. And we handle the majority of health-care claims transactions—tens of billions of them—in the United States.

We touch virtually every stakeholder in health care—physicians, manufacturers, hospitals, providers, and consumers. That's a big universe of stakeholders. In fact, we are unique in the breadth and depth of services we offer to health care. We want to keep them happy, and we want to serve their needs better than anyone else can.

I think most of us would agree that innovation happens close to the customer. The better we understand what our market wants, the better we understand what our current customers and our potential customers need; and the closer we are to their world, the better we can apply our unique perspective to see the gaps between what is and what could be.

Typically, a company's relationships with its customers happen far away from IT. They happen close to sales, close to marketing, and close to customer service, but far from IT. That perceived distance can be a disadvantage for IT.

How does IT overcome that disadvantage? I would submit to you that we can take on a consulting role—if we develop the capability, the intimacy with the business, and the awareness of the key business drivers that earns us a seat at the planning table. Then we can work side by side with business leaders to craft solutions that will help the business prosper and grow.

Those solutions, in many instances, will be the result of experiments. That's how innovation occurs, through experimentation. We aren't talking about massive IT projects or multiyear, multimillion-dollar initiatives, we're talking about experiments with mobile devices, with tablets, with cloud services, with social media.

But here's a critical point: IT isn't going to control those experiments tightly. Instead IT will participate, advise, and consult. Most important, IT will be aware of the hundred or so experiments that are happening at the same time across the entire span of the business and will begin threading common technologies through those experiments, linking them to existing systems, building or leveraging common platforms, and minimizing rework and reinvention.

For example, at McKesson we saw more than 20 different development organizations that were each beginning to experiment with mobile computing. By being aware of and helping with these experiments, we were able to put together a single mobility infrastructure and a mobile platform development team that allowed each of the businesses to participate fully and at very low cost, instead of mounting their own one- or two-person development capability or outsourcing that capability somewhere else.

Over and over again, we see that our presence in these businesses, through direct relationship management, through ties into their strategic planning organizations, allows us to encourage and support innovation across the company.

Some of those innovations become real products and services, and they create a competitive edge. When they become truly successful, they are likely duplicated by competitors, and eventually they begin to look more like commodities. During this evolution, IT's job shifts from innovation enablement to operational rigor, and then finally to compressing the costs out and operating at the highest level of efficiency possible.

By embracing that cycle and allocating part of its effort toward each segment of the cycle, IT continually feeds the business and helps it thrive.

This isn't magic. It's discipline—the same discipline required to manage any successful business. You make sure that you're collaborating with the stakeholders at every level. You make sure that you have good governance in place so that you can tie these efforts together across the many divisions of your organization. You make sure you have the right talent and capabilities for each of the jobs to be done. And you make sure you operate at competitive levels of cost and quality.

But you cannot possibly sit at that table unless you have established your credibility. If you can't demonstrate the ability to execute well on basic IT functions, you aren't going to be seen as a credible leader. The best path to credibility is by operating IT like a business. Measure what you do, relentlessly apply the basic principles and leadership concepts of any service organization. Experiment, learn, and, when necessary, kill your experiments quickly. Move with velocity and confidence and humility.

I came into the job of CIO seven years ago. I'm probably the only CIO of a Fortune 15 company who had never been a CIO before. I was running several of our health-care technology businesses when our CEO asked me to apply the same principles we used in the businesses to the IT function. He wanted me to run IT like a business.

The first thing I did was try to figure out who my customers were. The customers were the 12 major divisions of McKesson. I brought together the presidents of those organizations and formed a governance board, and then brought together the IT leaders of those organizations and set up a CIO council. We then brought in their key technologists and set up a technology council. Essentially I said, "My job is enabling you. I need to be working on what you need."

We turned IT into an organization that exists to fulfill IT demand. By working together across each of our businesses, and by holding ourselves accountable to the presidents and IT leaders of each of the organizations, and by planning only in collaboration, never in conflict, we were able to achieve some pretty dramatic results on every front. At the same time, the maturity of governing other shared services also expanded, and our presidents now oversee more than $3 billion of shared expense through this overall governance process.

Unquestionably, new technologies are important. We need to master and manage them. But the real challenge for IT is building new capability, leadership talent, business relevance, connections, and relationships with business leaders. IT needs to stay on top of the trends and shifts impacting the company and its customers. That's how IT delivers value to the modern enterprise: by understanding how to help it prosper and grow in a continually changing world.

—Randy Spratt
EVP, CIO, and CTO
McKesson Corporation

ACKNOWLEDGMENTS

This is my third book, and like its predecessors, it is primarily a work of collected knowledge. The concepts and frameworks contained in this book are derived primarily from the experience that I acquired over three decades as a consultant in the IT industry. But this book also represents two years of persistent research, involving dozens of interviews. I could not have completed this book without leveraging the collective wisdom of many expert sources. I thank them sincerely for their time, their energy, their intelligence, and their generosity.

I am deeply grateful to Rich Adduci, Thaddeus Arroyo, Bruce Bachenheimer, Ramón Baez, Linda Ban, Puneet Bhasin, Whitney Bouck, Greg Buoncontri, Tim Campos, Mike Capone, Tim Crawford, Sameer Dholakia, Tim Dilley, John Engates, Carol Fawcett, Jay Ferro, Thomas Fountain, Peter High, Kim Hammonds, Doug Harr, Donagh Herlihy, Daphne E. Jones, Sheila B. Jordan, Mike Kail, Jim Knight, Dr. William R. LaFontaine, Jonathan Landon, Françoise LeGoues, Ralph Loura, Tony Leng, Arthur McAdams, Chris McGugan, Todd McKinnon, Michael Minelli, Gordon Payne, Don Peppers, Steve Phillips, Mark Polansky, Bruce Rosenstein, Bill Ruh, Brian Queenin, Doug Schneider, Tony Scott, Frank Slootman, Dave Smoley, Randy Spratt, Tim Stanley, Kimberly Stevenson,

Don Tapscott, Patricia Titus, Jim Tosone, John Yapaola, and Tony Zingale.

While researching and writing this book, I received invaluable assistance and ongoing support from my colleagues at HMG Strategy: Cathy Fell, Kristen Liu, Melissa Marr, and Amanda Vlastas.

I also extend my sincere thanks to Sheck Cho and Stacey Rivera, my editors at John Wiley & Sons, who had faith in the value of the project and were patient when I missed my deadlines.

I owe a special debt of gratitude to Mike Barlow, the coauthor of *Partnering with the CIO* (Wiley, 2007) and *The Executive's Guide to Enterprise Social Media Strategy* (Wiley, 2011). Mike served as project manager for this book, and his guidance was truly invaluable. In addition to being a talented writer and editor, Mike is a genuinely nice guy. Thank you, Mike!

Most of all, I want to thank my wife, Sandra, and our two sons, Chase and Brice, who put up with long nights of writing, endless phone calls, and lost weekends of heavy editing.

INTRODUCTION

If you believe, as I do, that technology is a primary driver of wealth and prosperity, then it's hard to imagine a better time to be alive. Yes, we are living in a time of great change. But much of the change we see around us is genuinely positive. People are living longer, enjoying their families more, and spending more time following their passions. When you take an inventory of the pros and the cons of modern life, there's no question that we're better off today than we were 100 years ago.

Our health, our material wealth, and our leisure time can all be traced back to technological innovation. In truth, it's hard to overestimate the positive impact of technology on our world.

But all change requires credible leadership. When good leadership is in place, innovation follows. Innovation sets the stage for transformation. Leadership, innovation, and transformation aren't merely words. They are stages in a natural process of change and evolution that elevates us, as individuals and as organizations.

One of the main reasons that I love my job is because it enables me to meet regularly with the world's top CIOs and IT leaders. Talking to brilliant people, listening to their stories, and sharing ideas is inspiring and fulfilling.

As human beings, we learn by sharing stories. Like my previous two books, this book is essentially a collection of stories told by extremely bright people at the peaks of their careers. I truly believe that the work we do at my firm, HMG Strategy, is part of a larger process by which critical information is shared and distributed across a global network of people united by a genuine passion for elevating the role of information technology.

We've reached an interesting moment in the history of IT. Everyone seems to agree that information technology is important and indispensable. But there is a growing debate over which part of the enterprise should be in charge of information technology. The debate isn't trivial. Careers are at stake, to be sure. But perhaps more important, a new vision of the future is crystallizing. The modern enterprise is reshaping and transforming itself into something new and different.

The role of the CIO in that transformed enterprise isn't entirely clear. What does seem clear, however, is our collective responsibility to define that role, explore its potential, and map its dimensions.

I strongly believe that the CIO must be a leader of innovation and transformation, and not a follower. As a group, CIOs have knowledge and experience that are exceptional and unique. Who else but the CIO can "see" across every functional unit and division of the enterprise, understanding and perceiving all of the technology that enables the modern corporation to survive?

I urge CIOs to embrace change and become proactive champions of continuous transformation. CIOs have earned their seats at the executive table. Now we need to show the world what we can do.

The key to becoming a successful leader in any business is understanding the business. By understanding their business, CIOs can use that knowledge to create the optimal alignment of technology and strategy.

Ideally, CIOs should understand their company's customers and competitors even better than the company's chief marketing officers and vice presidents of sales understand the company's customers and competitors. CIOs with deep knowledge of external markets are well positioned to talk strategy with their peers in the C-suite.

Additionally, CIOs should focus more on bringing innovation to market. Innovating within IT generally creates efficiencies and reduces costs. Innovating for external markets, however, has the potential to produce revenue and increase shareholder value. From my perspective, strong CIOs focus on both internal and external innovation. Focusing on external innovation means focusing on the needs and desires of customers.

The Other Side of the Firewall: Understanding Your Company's Markets

Do you have a clear understanding of your company's markets? Do you know what customers want and what drives value on the other side of the firewall?

Those are the kinds of questions that should be keeping you up at night. By now, most of the critical technology challenges—the daily blocking and tackling—should be under control and manageable. Today's successful CIOs focus on creating value and driving business growth. They are more than stewards of the company's IT investments—they are innovators, pioneers, and transformational leaders of the epic revolution. They build open and trusting relationships across the C-suite, enjoy truly bidirectional dialogues with their peers, and keep watch on what's going on in the world outside.

Their primary focus has shifted from internal to external. They scour the Internet for news about changes in markets. They know how the competition leverages technology, and they make sure that their IT team is ready to support similar or better technology. They scout the horizon for new ideas and innovations that can be put to use to create competitive advantages. They are no longer the people who keep the servers running—they are the men and women who help the company stay ahead of the pack in a hypercompetitive global economy.

In other words, they are leaders. They are indispensable executives with skin in the game. Their success is measured in economic terms, rather than in purely technical terms.

Earnings per share is their key metric, and their performance is judged by their ability to work smoothly and effectively with the C-suite to achieve the company's strategic goals.

Again, it all comes down to focus. If the focus is internal, the best you can hope for is an IT shop that delivers great service to the enterprise. But when the focus is external, the sky is the limit. CIOs who understand the needs of their companies' external customers are worth their weight in gold. They are the transformational leaders who support collaboration and communication across business silos to deliver fabulous service and great products to external markets and external customers. They fundamentally understand the economics of capitalism. On a deep level, they understand the truth of how business works. They know in their hearts that markets and customers—the people who live outside the firewall—determine which companies succeed and which fail.

The modern CIO did not spring into existence overnight. Today's CIO is the result of three decades of evolution. It seems entirely natural that the CIO's focus has shifted from internal to external. Outside is where the money lives. If you believe in following the money, it makes perfect sense to keep your eyes and ears trained on what's going on in the world around you.

It's All about People

CIOs must also strive to become trusted partners and consultants to the business. CIOs must inspire confidence, through words and actions. Most of all, CIOs must be champions of people.

When the people are on your side, anything is possible. Technology will get cheaper, faster, and more powerful. But it will never fully replace people. Having the right people will make you; having the wrong people will break you.

Do you have a strong team? Have you surrounded yourself with smart people? Have you earned their trust and loyalty? Have you provided the strategy, direction, guidance, leadership, and mentoring they need to elevate their game and produce superior results? Do they have your support? Have you given them the freedom they need to succeed?

I believe that people will always trump technology. That's why I write books about people. As it happens, the people I write about are executives whose jobs involve making decisions about technology. I am fascinated by their stories, their insights, and their opinions. I hope that you enjoy this book and find it a valuable source of new ideas.

Making the Case for Continuous Business Transformation

As I mentioned, this is a book of stories and anecdotes. The style of my writing is conversational and informal. I think that's the best approach for a modern business book. I would like to begin by recounting a conversation I had recently with Mike Hill.

Mike has been with IBM for 35 years, and like many other executives at IBM, he has held a variety of positions within the company. His current title is vice president of enterprise initiatives. Essentially, Mike leads a team that is responsible for taking new ideas with great potential and building them into businesses that can be rolled back into the core IBM business.

In the past year, I have interviewed Mike several times. Each time we've spoken, he has shared valuable insights gathered over the course of his long career. In one of the interviews, I asked Mike to explain how a large company like IBM pursues a strategy of continuous innovation and transformation. Here's a condensed version of what he told me:

> *We know a lot about transformational leadership here at IBM. We've been on a path of continuous transformation for the past 20 years. We can execute on our strategies today because we transformed—and continue to transform—our organization and our businesses. We take the idea of transformational leadership very seriously.*

I really appreciate how Mike makes the case for an integrated approach to leadership, innovation, and transformation. Here is another portion from our conversation about leadership:

> *We are in a new era. Today's markets are dynamic and volatile. Traditional leadership models can't keep up with the accelerating pace of change. Remaining competitive requires continuous business transformation and tight operational alignment. CIOs are perfectly positioned to provide the guidance, expertise, and leadership needed to navigate smoothly, safely, and effectively through this new and exciting world.*

Our experience with cloud computing here at IBM is a good example of the kind of transformation and alignment that creates a path for success. For many years, we had relied on our Business Leadership Model to create and nurture new businesses within IBM. That model of developing and supporting new businesses had proved very successful for us.

But when we looked at the cloud, we saw as a multibillion-dollar business opportunity, and we knew that we needed a different kind of model to bring that business to fruition. Sam Palmisano, who was our CEO from 2000 to 2011, created a new strategy team called Enterprise Initiatives. That's the team that I lead. Our mission is taking new ideas with great potential and building them into businesses that can be rolled back into the core IBM business.

What does that mean? It means watching over them, developing their portfolios, protecting their funding, and driving initial sales. It means helping them scale up and nurturing their leadership. Our job is building and installing all the plumbing that those new ventures will need to survive and succeed in a fiercely competitive business environment.

For Sam and his successor, Ginni Rometty, it made perfect sense to create and support an innovative approach for building and scaling new initiatives within IBM. They truly believe in transformational leadership, and their business decisions reflect that sincere commitment.

From my perspective, it seems clear that leadership, innovation, and transformation are inextricably woven together. They are strands of a larger tapestry, and they are absolutely critical to the continuing success of organizations such as IBM.

I asked Mike for his perspective on the current state of cloud computing, since that is also one of his passions. Here is what he told me:

Sometimes I worry about the word "cloud," because it makes people think of something magical. But there's nothing really magical about cloud computing. It won't suddenly make your company more agile or your IT team more efficient.

Cloud computing can be very useful, and it offers many tangible benefits to the modern business. But the cloud represents a genuine change from the past, and as we all know, change is always difficult. Change takes years, and it involves real work. There are no magic wands or incantations to speed the process along. You've got to map your existing systems and infrastructure onto a new frame of reference, and that takes time and effort.

The cloud grid is different from the legacy grid. It's a whole new world, complete with peril and opportunity. Getting there requires leadership, and CIOs will play a huge role in the transformation from legacy to cloud computing.

In my current role, I am responsible for delivering the 2015 P&L [profit and loss] roadmap for cloud computing within IBM. From our perspective, the cloud is an integrated value proposition, not just a set of parts. So we put together a team to drive our cloud initiatives, and my job is leading the team.

We don't expect cloud computing to replace traditional computing in the near term. We expect that in 2015, about 90 percent of the typical IT budget will be spent on legacy systems. But we expect to see more and more cloud-enabled and cloud-centric workloads. Our research shows that moving workloads into the cloud can generate greater efficiency and agility. We're betting that when businesses see the potential value in cloud computing, they will naturally gravitate toward it.

That gravitational attraction will surely have an impact on CIOs. Faced with demands for greater agility, faster turnarounds, and lower costs, CIOs will naturally look to the cloud for potential answers. They will also look to other promising technologies, such as mobile, social, and big data analytics. Harnessing all of those newer technologies, and making sure they work together effectively to produce real business results, will require transformational leadership.

At the end of one of our conversations, Mike reminded me that even the greatest of strategies can fail unless you have also got great execution. In the final analysis, execution is what counts. In an era of continuous change and rapid evolution, the ability to execute on a vision is the key to success. From my perspective, the role of the CIO in leading innovation and transformation change has never been more important.

Chapter 1

The Innovation Challenge

A brilliant editor once told me that all news is local. In other words, unless the news has a direct impact on you or someone you know, it is largely irrelevant.

His observation also applies to IT innovation. A new tool or solution qualifies as innovation when it delivers a tangible benefit that helps you perform a task or achieve an objective faster, better, and more cost effectively than before. When it does not deliver a tangible benefit that leads to some kind of measurable improvement, I do not think it qualifies as innovation.

It is quite possible that a particular innovation can deliver tangible benefits to some people and to some organizations, but not to all people and to all organizations. And it is also quite possible that a particular innovation might be great for a large organization, but prove impractical for a small organization.

If you accept the idea that innovation has to provide some tangible benefit, it becomes apparent that global innovation does not necessarily translate into local innovation. Scale and location matter. They are variables that must be taken into account when considering the potential value of innovative projects.

My research into innovation has convinced me that successful innovation models are complex and multidimensional. They are neither simple nor linear. Like physics, innovation seems to work differently at different ends of the scale. As a result, small organizations and large organizations are likely to approach innovation in different ways.

Innovation can appear dramatic or mundane. It can be sustaining or disruptive. It can have a large audience or a small audience. It can result in high-margin gains or low-margin gains. It can be embraced and adopted quickly, or over time.

Will a standard model for innovation emerge? Possibly, but it will not be a simple model. It will look more like a network or a bundle of synapses. It will not be reduced into a binary equation. In fact, I see at least six distinct capabilities required for continuous innovation in the modern enterprise:

1. **Multidirectionality.** The modern innovation model will take multiple paths and explore multiple options. It will combine internal and external resources. It will have focus and structure, but it is also flexible and resilient. It will assume a certain level of risk, with the understanding that risk is proportional to reward.

2. **Inside and outside balance.** Successful innovation strategies will leverage a blend of traditional research

and development (R&D) and external resources to find creative solutions and serve new markets.

3. **Redefined teams.** Innovation requires a different approach to team building. In the past, team members were selected for compatibility and skills. Modern innovation teams will include insiders and outsiders, people who can find and leverage the appropriate resources (whether external or internal), people who bring different views and opinions—people who might not even be considered "team players."

4. **Deep knowledge and market awareness.** Innovation also requires deep and extensive knowledge and awareness of the competitive landscape. You have to know what the competition is doing and know your competitor's business—even better than the competition knows its own business!

5. **Partnering with the world.** For serial innovators, everyone is a potential partner. You must find good ideas wherever they are, and figure out how to make them work within your ecosystem to create new value for your customers.

6. **Speed.** Technology and globalization have greatly reduced the length of modern business cycles. Everything is moving faster, and the time between cycles has shortened dramatically. Market-leading companies innovate continuously and quickly. Innovative organizations measure speed in two significant dimensions: speed to market and speed to failure. Both measures are critical. The faster you innovate, the faster

you get new products and services to market. But you can't have innovation without failure, and the best way to fail is to fail quickly.

The Psychology of Innovation

Throughout this book, we will examine the underlying traits and characteristics of leadership that result in innovation and transformation. We will slowly build a case for innovation leadership, and share the experiences of successful executives who have "been there, done that."

Based on our research, we've developed a table of characteristics that define leaders of innovation. The table is more descriptive than prescriptive; it is more of a menu than a recipe. But I think that now is the right time to share it with you. As you can see in Figure 1.1, I have divided the

Optimizer	Innovator
⬇	⬇
Right brain	Left brain
Recursive	Combinatorial
Habitual	Transcendent
Fast thinking	Slow thinking
Algorithmic	Heuristic
Risk averse	Risk taker
Puzzle solver	Paradigm shifter
Conservator	Value creator

Figure 1.1   Characteristics of Leadership

universe of CIOs and IT leaders into two camps: optimizers and innovators. It is an arbitrary division, since most of us live in both universes. But it serves as a method for contrasting the differences between two kinds of mindsets.

As my friend Daphne Jones, the CIO of Hospira, recently said, "Innovation is really a mindset." I truly believe that she is right. Innovation is a mindset, and a set of character traits. Innovation is a way of looking at the world. As Daphne would say, "Is your mindset flexible and dexterous, or is it fixed and closed?"

After chatting with Daphne, I realized that innovation really is a mindset. And that realization gives me great hope for the future, because mindsets can be changed.

An Expanding Range of Influence

My interviews and research also showed clearly that the CIO's traditional range of influence is expanding rapidly. In the past, the CIO's influence was limited to a thin slice of the organization. Now, thanks to the ubiquity of IT, the CIO's influence extends far and wide.

But greater influence confers greater responsibility. It is not enough to be influential—you have got to leverage your influence to help the enterprise grow and succeed.

Figure 1.2 shows the many circles in which the CIO exerts influence. It is an amazing testament to the growth of the CIO's role over the past two decades.

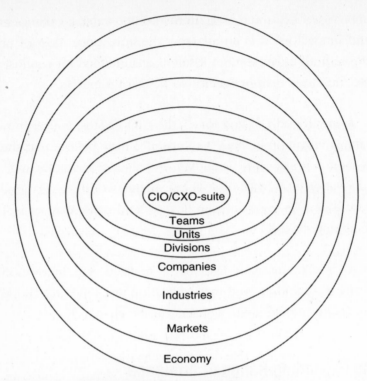

Figure 1.2　The CIO's Circles of Influence

Speed and Failure Are Essential in Continuous Innovation Strategies

The pharmaceutical industry, which depends on continuous innovation for its survival, understands the delicate relationship between speed, failure, and innovation—and has developed strategies for achieving success through failure.

Most pharmaceutical companies rely on a two-stage approach to innovation. In the primary stage, the emphasis is on discovery and testing. In the secondary stage, the focus shifts to success and refinement. The initial stage focuses on the abstract and the ideal, while the later stage zooms in on practical applications for real-world markets.

Both stages are necessary. The initial stage is where the failures take place. The later stage is where the product emerges. In the early stage, failure is not only acceptable, it is expected—because the whole purpose of the early stage is separating winners from losers. Only the winners are sent ahead to the later stage, where they are groomed and prepared for market success.

The innovation strategies used in the pharmaceutical business offer valuable lessons for all of us and are worthy of deeper study. I especially like the concept of a logical, repeatable process that begins with abstractions and ends with the creation of real products that generate measurable value for the enterprise.

If you want to learn more, I recommend a *Harvard Business Review* article entitled "A More Rational Approach to New-Product Development" (March 2008) by Eric Bonabeau, Neil Bodick, and Robert W. Armstrong.

It always helps to remember that innovation is both a combinatorial and a collaborative phenomenon. It does not happen in a vacuum, and you cannot do it alone.

That is why peer-to-peer interaction among CIOs and other IT leaders is essential for continuous innovation.

Fail Fast and Fail Smart

Back in the early days of the space race, it seemed as though the U.S. rockets were always blowing up. It turned out that many of the rockets launched by the Soviets had also blown up. But unlike the United States, which shared information about rocket launches with the public, the Soviets did not broadcast the results of their tests. As a result, most people never knew about their failures.

As anyone who has ever experimented with rockets knows, many launches end in failure. In rocketry, failure is accepted as a normal phase of the innovation process. You pick up the pieces, analyze what went wrong, and try to fix it. Most important, you keep testing.

We recently caught up with legendary marketing guru Don Peppers, the coauthor with Martha Rogers of *The One to One Future*[1] and *Extreme Trust*.[2] Don has a bachelor's degree in astronautical engineering from the U.S. Air Force Academy, so technically, he is a rocket scientist. His science background, combined with his graduate degree in public affairs from Princeton, gives him a truly unique perspective on the importance of continuous innovation in the modern economy.

"Great companies are always testing," says Don. "When you test, you invariably have hits and misses. Many of your hits are random. That's normal. So instead of focusing solely on outcomes, you should focus on inputs. Did you ask the right questions? Were the tests set up properly? Were there hidden biases? Then you're learning and moving forward, whether the end result was a hit or miss."

In other words, sometimes the questions can be more important than the answers. This is a critical takeaway for innovation leaders. The more you focus on results, the more likely you are to miss the big picture. The key trends are more important, and they should be the focus of your attention.

Reducing innovation to a simple binary process of separating winning ideas from losing ideas is unlikely to produce genuinely useful results over the long term. Innovation is an iterative process, and each step leads to another. Sometimes, you are not exactly sure where you are going—and that is okay, as long as you are learning and continually improving.

"While it isn't too hard to predict the general direction of innovation, the actual outcomes are often random," says Don. "Ten years ago, for instance, if you had predicted that Apple Computer would become the world's largest music retailer, or that Nokia would become the world's largest camera manufacturer, no one would have believed you. But even 10 years ago we all knew that it was inevitable that music and photographs would eventually be rendered in digital form and transmitted electronically."

Even a string of failures, if they provide enough learning, can lead to success. Before its highly successful iPod, Apple failed with a personal digital assistant called the Newton. And the United States won the space race by acknowledging failures early, then using the knowledge gained from those failures to develop systems and technologies significantly more advanced than the Soviets'.

The New Speed of Change

Greg Buoncontri has been CIO of Pitney Bowes (PB) since 2000. Prior to joining PB, Greg was CIO at Novartis Pharmaceuticals, and before that he was CIO at Sandoz Pharmaceuticals. Over a career spanning more than three decades, Greg has seen his share of change and transformation.

What has changed the most, however, is the speed of change. "You'd have to be living in a different universe not to recognize the accelerated rate at which things are happening across all kinds of spectrums, whether it's technology, business, politics, finance, or geopolitical affairs. It's incredible," says Greg. "Thinking back over my career and life, I honestly don't think I've seen anything like this before. This is truly unprecedented."

The speed at which innovative new products and services reach new or growing markets is particularly amazing, says Greg.

"Today, you have all kinds of innovation taking place. Some of it's good and some of it's bad. But there's no advantage in denying that innovation is happening all around us," he says. "Sometimes I hear people talking about wanting to survive this time of transition. I think just the opposite. I want to thrive. Innovation creates white space that is filled with opportunity. Innovation isn't something you run away from. Innovation makes you better. It's a horse you want to ride. It might be difficult and challenging, but it's going to take you to a better place."

As most of you already know, PB built its reputation on innovation. The company's iconic postage meter transformed traditional mail, and PB has maintained a unique spirit of inventiveness since its founding in 1920.

"We have a really rich legacy of innovating across multiple channels," says Greg. "One of the ways we foster innovation is through a program called Idea-Net, which started a couple of years ago, where we encouraged employees to make suggestions for innovation around products, processes, customer experience, or internal processes. We collect ideas over the course of the year. There are governance groups that look at the ideas and then decide which ones they want to go forward with and they implement them. There are various ways in which we recognize the people or teams whose ideas have been adopted or implemented. It's been extremely successful."

PB has rightfully earned its reputation as a serial innovator. Although many people still fondly remember the company for its postage meter, PB now provides innovative software, hardware, and services that integrate physical and digital communications channels. The company has annual sales of about $5.3 billion and employs 29,000 people worldwide.

"When you look at our products and lines of business, you see a transformation from a purely physical world to a world that is increasingly digital," says Greg. "In our company, innovation is an ongoing process. It never stops. You need to have a culture and a process that recognizes that not all innovation is going to be successful. There might be failures. In fact, those failures produce learning. The companies that are really good at innovation are the ones that have reduced the cost of failure, which allows them to experiment and innovate more. We've always been an innovative company in our space. Now we're widening the space in which we innovate. This is a fascinating experience and a very exciting time."

Focus on the Business Challenge, Not on the Technology

Tim Campos is the CIO at Facebook. In many ways, he represents a new generation of CIOs who successfully combine business and technology skills to generate value for the enterprise. He studied electrical engineering and computer science at the University of California at Berkeley. He also holds an Executive MBA from an innovative program that combines the resources of Berkeley's Haas School of Business and Columbia Business School. Graduates of the bicoastal program receive two degrees, one from Berkeley and one from Columbia.

I am sure that Tim would have both diplomas hanging on the wall of his office, except that nobody at Facebook has an office—including legendary founder Mark Zuckerberg!

I think it is fair to say that Facebook is one of the most amazing success stories of the past decade. And like Facebook, Tim is something of a prodigy: At the age of 32, he was named CIO at KLA-Tencor and became the youngest CIO of a Fortune 500 company.

At Facebook, Tim has a bird's-eye view of the new relationship between IT and the enterprise. I asked him to tell me how the cloud was changing the role of the CIO in modern organizations. Here is a summary of what he told me:

There is so much involved in making technology work with traditional on-premise methodology. Any business decision that involves technology involves a whole bunch of other things that go along with that technology. You must have a data center. You must have a technical operations group. You must have an ability to monitor and maintain all of the technical infrastructure.

In a cloud-enabled world, you can get all of the benefits of technology without the investment in the data centers, the people, the infrastructure . . . and that changes the equation.

A cloud-based solution allows you to focus your management attention solely on applying technology to the business problem . . . and not on the bits and bytes and mechanics of the technology itself.

When you do that in scale—in other words, when you apply cloud as a strategy across your entire enterprise architecture—it's really transformative. At Facebook, for example, most of our internal information services are cloud-based services. That changes how we think about the IT function. And it changes what we get out of IT.

Younger companies that are growing up in this cloud-enabled world view IT very differently than traditional companies that have been around for 30 years but are the same size.

I asked Tim to compare the skill sets of traditional IT organizations and IT organizations that rely more on cloud-based services. Here's a sample of his reply:

When you're using cloud-based services, the skills you need are less technical and more business-oriented. Imagine a traditional IT function . . . you need database administration, systems administration . . . all these heavy IT skills that are not business related. You don't need all those skills in the IT organization when you're using cloud-based services. So almost by definition, you're more aligned with the business.

The cloud changes the nature of the relationship between IT and the business. It's easier for IT to be responsive to the business. Let's say you're using Salesforce.com and your business is growing fast. If the size of your sales organization doubles, you don't have to rethink your CRM application . . . you just have to add more licenses and let Salesforce.com make it work. Salesforce knows how to do this more effectively than any of us would by ourselves. And they have the economic incentive to figure it out.

If you're just using the cloud for one application, you probably won't see the benefits. But when you're using cloud for almost all of your applications, then it's a huge change.

We still have a very small percentage of the IT environment on-premise, so we can see the difference between the on-premise systems and the cloud systems.

The contrasts are striking. In the areas where we spend the most time, the areas where we experience the most pain (pain as defined by work output necessary relative to the business output that we get out), the benefit of the cloud systems becomes strikingly clear. You don't waste your time on things like upgrades and making sure that you have the newest patch revision and all of that.

I also asked Tim about security in the cloud. Here's what he told me:

I'd say there are two types of security issues. The first one is a myth and the second one is real. The first issue, which is a myth, is that these cloud solutions aren't secure. And that they would be less secure than your internal on-premise systems. I don't think there's any evidence of that. I don't think there's any evidence that Salesforce.com has continuously been compromised. But there's tons of evidence that enterprises are compromised every day because of accounts that don't get terminated or employees who take information from their companies for nefarious reasons. Those are the real security risks that we face on a daily basis. For a cloud provider to succumb to that on their production systems would mean death to the company. So they invest a tremendous amount in the security of their ecosystems. I don't think that the general security of these systems is a real issue.

But there is a secondary issue of data ownership, and that is real. For example, it is not possible for a company to say (in a way that meets certain commitments to external parties) that it owns its data if that data lives with a cloud provider. A very simple example would be user data. Let's say that you give certain guarantees about how you handle user data (i.e., when you say that it's deleted, that it's actually deleted, or that you will not give it to a third party, except under certain conditions). You can't make those guarantees about data that lives with somebody else, because you don't know how they're going to handle the data, even if they make that promise to you.

And there is a class of information for which encryption or some other solution is necessary in order for you to use the cloud. That does limit the cloud's utility in certain situations. There are plenty of examples of types of information for which a certain class of protection is necessary that a cloud service provider won't or can't provide to meet your requirements. Which means there are certain types of data that you don't want to put in the cloud.

I sincerely appreciate Tim's candor and insight. His observations are spot on. The cloud offers benefits—and drawbacks. As the CIO, you need to weigh the pros and cons, and reach a decision that makes sense for your IT organization and the larger enterprise it serves.

In the Modern Enterprise, True Innovation Takes Many Shapes and Forms

Over the past year, I have spoken with dozens of CIOs about their innovation strategies. One truth that has emerged clearly from our research is that innovation takes various shapes and forms. We tend to think about innovation in terms of new products, services, or processes. Sometimes, however, innovation can take the form of a new way of looking at things.

Several good examples of this surfaced during a recent conversation with Steve Phillips, senior vice president and CIO at Avnet, Inc. Steve told me that he believes IT is ideally positioned to support and champion innovation, especially for technology companies, because "IT teams that work closely with their business colleagues have a deep understanding of how business processes 'really' operate and the way that business processes and technology interact." Typically, IT teams can determine fairly rapidly if a new technology idea has a chance of evolving into a real product or service.

To encourage innovation, Avnet's IT team has an annual contest for its North American employees to encourage people to come forward with their ideas.

"We have something called the 'CIO Challenge' every year," says Steve. "We encourage all of our IT people to put their good ideas on the table. Typically, the best ideas that emerge aren't for new products, but for new ways to make IT more efficient and our company an even better place to work."

In 2012, more than 18 ideas were submitted, either by individuals or teams. Instead of the winner being solely selected by management, the ideas are reviewed by an employee council.

"The employee council sifts through every idea, and they pick the top three from their point of view," says Steve. "Then the entire IT team votes on the top three and picks a winner. My commitment as CIO is to support the winning idea. Typically, the ideas don't need a lot of investment, although I'll commit up to $50,000 if needed. More than anything else, usually, they need support from management and prioritization."

The most recent winning idea was the creation of an Ideas Laboratory, which involved setting up a small IT work team who could experiment part-time with new technologies and tools with a focus on how they could be used to deliver business value. In the prior year, the winning idea grew from the desire of some IT staff to learn more about the newer technologies being used in Avnet IT, such as Microsoft SharePoint or SAP.

Essentially, these employees did not want to be limited to the older technology they currently work with and wanted to consider alternative technology career tracks within Avnet. To provide them with this experience, Avnet created a "Technology Day," followed up by a job shadowing opportunity. Steve explains how it works:

It's a voluntary program for our IT employees, where they can spend a day learning from internal and external experts about the newer technologies being used at Avnet. This way, our people can better understand the kind of skills and opportunities open to them. At the end of the Technology Day, participants have the opportunity to sign up to shadow someone who works with the technology to learn even more about it. If they are still interested after that, the employee can say, "I'm interested in making a role transition here." There's no guarantee of a new role, but it's an opportunity to learn and express their interest. And if we can find a new role for these employees, then we do.

The Ideas Laboratory and Avnet Technology Day both demonstrate that innovation doesn't have to arrive in the form of a new product or service to generate useful business value. Sometimes a new process or a new approach can be just as valuable as a new application or device.

"The innovations that emerge from the CIO Challenge enhance and improve employee engagement," says Steve. "Higher levels of engagement often translate into higher levels of job satisfaction and productivity, which generate tangible business benefits."

The lesson here is that innovation comes in many shapes and sizes. A great innovation doesn't have to be a cool new app or sexy piece of hardware—what's important is whether it helps the business achieve its goals.

More information about Avnet's CIO Challenge can be found on Steve's blog *Behind the Firewall* (http://blogging .avnet.com/weblog/cioinsights).

Notes

1. Don Peppers and Martha Rogers, *The One to One Future: Building Relationships One Customer at a Time* (New York: Crown, 1993).

2. Don Peppers and Martha Rogers, *Extreme Trust: Honesty as a Competitive Advantage* (New York: Portfolio, 2012).

Chapter 2

Governance Trumps Process

When Ramón Baez became the CIO of Kimberly-Clark in February 2007, he didn't know that he would be personally involved in one of the great business comeback stories of the decade.

Like many companies, Kimberly-Clark was adversely affected by the economic crisis that began in 2008. By 2009, the company faced diminished prospects in several important markets. Chairman and CEO Thomas J. Falk rallied the company, calling for renewed focus in three critical areas: innovation, continuous improvement, and talent.

Confronting a clear need to innovate quickly, some companies might have created a complicated innovation process or simply outsourced innovation to consultants. Kimberly-Clark's approach was more original. Instead of adding more layers of complexity or hiring outside experts, the company relied on a governance committee to guide the innovation necessary for regaining the edge in competitive markets.

"The committee included the CEO, the group president of North Atlantic Consumer Products, the president of Kimberly-Clark International, and the chief marketing officer," explains Ramón. "Those four senior executives had to be in agreement before an innovation project went forward."

When the committee spoke, it spoke in one voice. That created a heightened sense of clarity across the company, which in turn made it easier to move projects from the ideation stage to the execution phase with greater speed and efficiency.

That unique form of governance also enabled the company to achieve alignment across multiple operating units and overcome internal obstacles that can derail or impede innovation.

The committee, which became known as the Innovation Council, met weekly during the economic downturn. Some of the innovations championed by the committee resulted in new or improved products. Some of the innovations involved new approaches to packaging or marketing.

The critical element, says Ramón, was that the company was not innovating in a vacuum. When the committee approved a project, it meant that all the potential benefits and liabilities had been carefully considered, and that senior management was on board.

The results speak for themselves. Today, Kimberly-Clark has approximately 57,000 employees worldwide, operations in 36 countries, and annual sales of about \$20.8 billion. It is again considered a leader in innovation and a model of success in global markets.

I believe that Kimberly-Clark's approach is truly brilliant. It is a genuinely innovative strategy for continuous innovation. The company's experience can also teach us valuable lessons about managing through a crisis. I am sure there was a temptation to tighten up on existing innovation processes and outsource as much as possible. Instead, the company improvised a unique strategy that was both successful and sustainable.

There is a huge difference between governance and process. Governance implies coordinated guidance and approval from the top. Governance sets the tone and sends a clear signal. Governance assigns responsibility and accountability.

Process, however, is just a series of steps, rules, and guidelines. Given a choice, I will take governance over process any day, especially when the stakes are high and the competition is fierce.

On a personal note, I would like to congratulate Ramón for his appointment as the new CIO of Hewlett-Packard (HP). Ramón was a great CIO at Kimberly-Clark, and I'm certain that he will be a great CIO at HP. Best of luck to you, Ramón!

Being a Leader of Innovation at an Innovative Enterprise

I recently asked Tony Scott, the CIO at Microsoft Corp., for his opinion on the qualities required for leading innovation at a company that is globally respected for developing and marketing innovative products and services.

We had a wide-ranging conversation, but one of his answers really stuck with me. He said that if you want to be an effective senior-level executive at a global enterprise, you need to be "brutally honest." He did not mean that you have to be rude or bully people. He meant that you have to speak the truth, even when it is difficult.

"It's easy to hide behind IT-speak," says Tony. "But it's a temptation you must avoid. You cannot build your own credibility unless you are brutally honest, even when being honest means acknowledging your own faults or shortcomings."

Tony recalled a situation in which all the reporting indicated that work related to an IT project was moving ahead satisfactorily. When another senior executive warned that some users were dissatisfied with aspects of the project, it would have been easy for Tony to have referred to the positive reports and overridden the executive's warning. Instead, the project was reviewed more carefully and the problems that had been identified by the users were addressed before they became major issues.

The ability and the willingness to acknowledge and fix problems quickly is a hallmark of innovative companies. Great executives like Tony know that it's better to fail early and fail fast. That's where "brutal honesty" becomes a competitive advantage.

Companies that identify and fix problems quickly will get high-quality products to market faster than companies that get slowed down by internal squabbles over who dropped the ball or who's to blame. Winning in today's markets requires genuine speed—being third or fourth makes you irrelevant.

I really like how Tony relates honesty to speed. It's almost as if honesty serves as a lubricant or an accelerator. Honesty gets you to the right solution faster—it enables victory.

Dishonesty, especially the kind that is bred by fear of failure, acts like friction. Even when it is unintentional, dishonesty weighs you down and makes it harder to cross the finish line ahead of the competition.

I am delighted that Tony took the time to share his wisdom with us. Microsoft is a company that lives and breathes innovation. The IT team plays a vital role in supporting the culture of innovation that enables the company to remain a world leader in today's ultracompetitive global economy.

Great Companies Avoid the "Me Too" Syndrome When Innovating

One way to generate innovation is by combining two or more existing products to create a new product. The best example of this approach to innovation is the iPhone, which is essentially a brilliant combination of many existing technologies packaged into a stylish slab of glass, metal, and plastic.

Another path to innovation is identifying a capability— something you already do really well—and creating an entirely new product from it.

A great example of that type of innovation is the ADP National Employment Report. Created by ADP in partnership with Macroeconomic Advisers, the report is derived from actual payroll data and measures the change in total nonfarm private employment each month.

I spoke recently with Mike Capone, ADP's corporate vice president of product development and chief information officer. Combining a unique blend of client-facing operational experience and strong technical knowledge, Mike guides both product development and information technology for ADP.

He estimates that about 70 percent of his time is spent on innovation. Although it originated before his time as CIO, he's especially proud of the ADP National Employment Report, which analyzes economic data collected by the company to generate highly usable business intelligence.

"The report contains the kind of information that moves markets," says Mike. "Unlike government reports, which are often based on surveys and samples, our report is based on actual payroll data. We can look at all of the data and see who's really hiring. Our reports tend to be very accurate."

Because of their accuracy, the reports are now considered an indispensable source of crucial business information. That's an amazing feat for an organization that built its reputation as a data processing company. The success of the new product was partly due to the company's willingness to think boldly and creatively.

"Anyone can do analytics. We decided to create something truly unique and valuable," says Mike. "For us, it wasn't about trying to do something that everyone else was already doing. We looked for something that would be genuinely different."

I love how Mike and his team at ADP moved quickly beyond the "me too" mindset and instead focused on creating a new product that would differentiate the company from everyone else in the market.

Notice how the goal was not "innovation" in some abstract sense—the goal was a specific product that would help the company. "At ADP, we produce lots of patents, but we're not interested in generating a bunch of patents just so we can say that we have a bunch of patents. If you focus first on innovation, patents will come and more importantly, our clients will benefit," says Mike.

I asked Mike if ADP has a formula or a process for innovating. Here's what he told me:

It's hard to put innovation in a box. We do have ADP labs. They come up with an idea, and then figure out how to productize it rapidly. We also use crowdsourcing within the company, and occasionally we hire third-party consultants. It really depends on the topic. We give our people lots of freedom in terms of how they approach innovation, how they go at it. Fail fast is our primary guideline. Try it out; if it doesn't work, throw it away. We don't punish people if their ideas don't work. And when they're successful, we try to give them some recognition. In the IT world, recognition means a lot.

There are some wonderful lessons here, and I'm delighted that Mike shared his experiences and insight with us.

Cycles of Innovation and Adoption

Randy Spratt, who wrote the foreword for this book, is executive vice president, CIO, and CTO at San Francisco–based McKesson Corp., a $112 billion enterprise providing services and products across the global healthcare economy.

I've known Randy for many years, and I included an interview with him in my previous book, *On Top of the Cloud*.[1] In that interview, Randy painted a picture of the typical IT value creation cycle, in which the company swung back and forth—much like a pendulum—between a state of "business nirvana" and "IT nirvana."

In the IT nirvana, everything is standardized and locked down. In the business nirvana, agility and innovation reign supreme.

The IT nirvana is all about efficiency, and the business nirvana is all about responding quickly—and profitably—to customer needs. An imaginary pendulum swings back and forth between the two nirvanas, which are forever separated. (See Figures 2.1 and 2.2.)

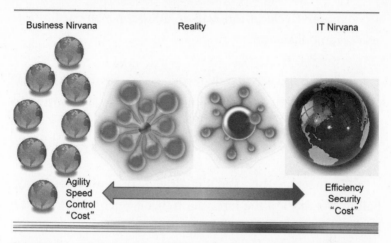

Figure 2.1 IT Life Cycle in Value Creation: Perpetual Pendulum

Randy wondered what would happen if the pendulum was replaced by a virtuous cycle. What would happen if efficiency and innovation were seen as two sides of the same coin, instead of two competing worldviews? The dualist notion suggested by the pendulum would be discarded in favor of

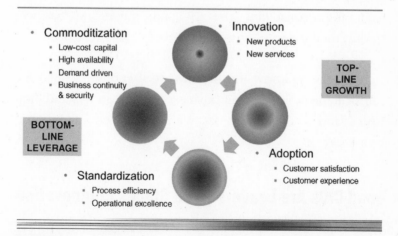

Figure 2.2 IT Life Cycles—Another Version: Virtuous Cycle

a continuous cycle of innovation, adoption, standardization, and commoditization.

I really like the way Randy identifies the dilemma and offers an elegant solution. I also think that Randy's vision of a virtuous cycle of efficiency and innovation deserves more study. It could very likely be the basis for a new model of CIO leadership.

"CIOs need to become the drivers of innovation," says Randy. But most of the innovation that is really valued by the business happens close to the customer. Driving innovation means getting closer to the company's customers. For some CIOs, getting close to customers will be a challenge. But Randy is confident that successful CIOs will figure out the best ways to balance efficiency and innovation.

Finding the right balance can be difficult, but it is not impossible. In some situations, the CIO can play a consultative role in the innovation process. By serving as an in-house technology consultant, the CIO can guide the business toward the best solutions—and prevent costly mistakes.

"We have to know the business well enough so that we can sit at the table with our business leaders, understand their issues, and work side by side with them to craft solutions," says Randy.

Good CIOs Are Leaders at All Stages of Innovation

"Successful CIOs participate across all stages of the cycle, from cutting-edge experimentation to early adoption, then to widespread adoption, and then to true commoditization," says Randy. "The pundits who predicted the end of the CIO role saw the CIO as someone who primarily manages the end stage of the cycle, the commoditization stage at which the goal is leveraging economies of scale. But good CIOs are leaders at each stage of the cycle, not just at the end. And they're making a difference."

It is also critical for CIOs to make the connection between the sharply rising demand for mobile apps and the growth of cloud usage. "The adoption of cloud has really been capitalized and propelled by the desire for mobile apps. As consumers and workers ask for more and more mobile capabilities on their devices of choice, it's pushing more applications into the cloud," says Randy.

This unexpected linkage of two apparently separate phenomena is certain to have major implications for CIOs.

"For a long time it was hard for most people to see the real value of cloud computing because the hype was ahead of the reality," says Randy. "Now the demand for mobile apps is driving cloud adoption and creating a whole new cycle of innovation."

At many companies, for example, mobile apps are used mostly by the sales team. At McKesson, however, the use of mobile apps has spread across various parts of the company. "In addition to helping our sales force with everyday mobility issues, we're doing some really cutting-edge stuff with mobile apps," says Randy. "Our radiology imaging group actually rewrote some of the graphics drivers on the iPad so they could effectively manipulate 3D CT scans for radiologists. Now the radiologists have a great new tool for communicating with their patients and showing them what's going on. It's an example of a new technology that doesn't exist anywhere else yet."

Today, we are seeing what Randy describes as a "hyper-velocity" of experimentation. Many of those experiments will fail, but some will lead to products and services that generate real value.

"Some of the experiments will make it into the mainstream. For that reason, it's not only very important for us to understand what many of the new capabilities can bring to us, but also to understand the inherent life spans of those new technologies and be anticipating when they're going to no longer serve their intended purpose, or when replacements or better alternatives will arise," says Randy. "We'll need to manage all the stages of the technology life cycle. That's the future of IT leadership."

From Enabler to Innovator: The Evolving Image of the CIO

I had a great conversation with Rich Adduci recently. As many of you know, Rich is senior vice president and CIO at Boston Scientific Corp., the worldwide developer, manufacturer, and marketer of medical devices. With approximately 25,000 employees and about $8 billion in annual revenue, BSC is highly regarded for continuous innovation and leadership.

During our conversation, I asked Rich about the CIO's unique ability to look across the modern global enterprise and get a bird's-eye view from top to bottom.

"Apart from the CEO, the CIO is mostly likely to have the widest and deepest perspective of the business and all of its various components," says Rich. "CIOs are uniquely positioned to identify challenges, promote solutions, and drive change."

Because we live in a digitally networked world, most of the transformational change that we experience involves some kind of technology. Ideally, the CIO should be perceived as a natural leader in innovation. But that's not always the case.

"Traditionally, most people associate IT with technical expertise. To the outside world, we are enablers. We automate processes and we help the company increase its efficiency," says Rich.

For IT, the challenge is going beyond that traditional image. Ideally, IT should be perceived as the go-to team for knowledge, insight, advice, and innovation.

"That means getting in front of the business and presenting new ideas," says Rich. "It means proactively identifying challenges and opportunities, developing solutions, and providing leadership."

The new scenario that Rich describes requires a CIO who is more business savvy and less risk averse than past generations of IT leaders. "If you're the CIO, you have to ask yourself, 'How can I make a difference?' You cannot wait for someone to ask you to build something. You need to step up and become the agent of change. There are plenty of opportunities if you actively look for them. The global economy is truly a target-rich environment for innovation," says Rich.

That is especially true in the healthcare industry, where every modern nation faces similar pressures to deliver healthcare more effectively and more efficiently than ever before.

"In our sector of the economy, the speed of change is astonishing," says Rich. "As a result, IT can make a profound impact on the value chain by helping to integrate services, driving down costs, improving outcomes, and building better relationships with providers and patients."

I love how Rich paints a picture of a world overflowing with opportunities for IT leaders who are ready to grab the ball and run with it. "As CIOs, we need to focus on solving big problems," he says. "We need to be leaders, not order takers. We have to decide to make a difference."

Replacing Up and Down with Left to Right

I spoke recently with Sameer Dholakia, group vice president and general manager, Cloud Platforms Group at Citrix Systems. Sameer and his colleagues at Citrix have an uncommon perspective on the organization of IT assets. Instead of seeing information moving up and down a series of stacks, they see it moving left to right across networks of integrated systems.

I love the image of information traveling left to right as opposed to up and down. In the left-to-right model, the leftmost point is the end user or customer. Everything flows from the user. Or looking at it from a purely IT perspective, everything to the right of the user is technology required to meet the user's needs.

"When you think left to right, it's impossible not to consider the megatrends impacting the user," says Sameer. "From the user's perspective, for example, mobility is critical. You need access to all your data and all your apps, wherever you are, whenever you need them."

As a cloud infrastructure software provider, Citrix naturally sees the cloud as a key element of global mobility. Sameer describes a flow of information from a user's personal cloud to data centers running in private or public clouds. It's really a network of clouds providing a seamless continuum of services to the user. "When you think of IT from an end-user perspective, with information flowing left to right instead of up and down, it all makes sense."

Sameer does not think the stack concept will become extinct in the near future, however. "Having a stack in the data center is fine," he says. "But the data center should not be viewed in isolation from the other technology services required by the user. The data center itself is part of the left-to-right flow."

My instinct tells me that it will be important for CIOs and other IT leaders to grasp the concept of left-to-right flow with the user at the starting point, and adjust their IT strategies accordingly. The up-and-down stack makes sense for the fundamental, heavy-lifting operations that are essential to providing IT services. But meeting the needs of increasingly sophisticated and tech-savvy users is another story—a story that just might be written left to right.

"Until recently, our main focus as IT leaders has been on the data center infrastructure and the services running there," says Sameer. "Now we also have to focus on the customers, the people using the services we provide. That's a change from the past, but it's a change we have to make."

Creating a Culture of Innovation

One of the most fascinating things we learned as we researched this book is that many of the executives whom we interviewed reacted generally positively to the term "culture of innovation" and generally negatively to the term "process of innovation."

When we asked them specifically which was more important, a culture of innovation or a process of innovation, virtually everyone we interviewed chose culture over process. A handful of executives told us that you need both.

I agree that you need both. But I also believe that you need the right structures and processes in place first, because it is those structures and processes that give rise to innovation.

In other words, I do not believe that innovation arises spontaneously. It does not appear suddenly of thin air; there must be preexisting conditions.

Our research leads me to believe that the most innovative organizations have the structures and processes necessary to support and nurture innovation in place and enabled.

Converting Ideas into Successful New Products and Services

It is all well and good for senior executives to urge employees to let their creative juices flow and spend more time "thinking out of the box." We've all attended meetings where someone says, "What we need here is some real innovation!"

But what actually happens when employees or business partners come up with great ideas? Where do they go? Who do they talk to get support or funding? How does the organization turn great ideas into commercially successful products and services?

I think of structures and processes as conveyor belts that move ideas through all the stages of development between concept and delivery.

Structures and processes turn ideas into new products and services, at the speed of modern business. If you are turning ideas into new products and services on a regular basis, you have got a culture of innovation.

When people talk about Apple as a world-class organization, they tend to focus on Steve Jobs or the company's reputation for discipline and secrecy.

While there is no question that Steve's vision was essential to Apple's success, I think the real key was Steve's unique understanding of how companies innovate. Steve met with his executive management team every Monday. He met with his marketing and communication team every Wednesday. He kept the meetings focused on results, and he held people directly accountable for their work.

Simplicity was the watchword. Here's a brief passage from Adam Lashinsky's excellent article in the May 23, 2011, issue of *Fortune* magazine:

> *The [Apple] org chart is deceptively straightforward, with none of the dotted-line or matrixed responsibilities popular elsewhere in the corporate world. There aren't any committees at Apple, the concept of general management is frowned on, and only one person, the chief financial officer, has a "P&L," or responsibility for costs and expenses that lead to profits or losses.*
>
> *At most corporations today, having a P&L is considered a badge of honor. At Apple, however, P&Ls are apparently*

seen as distractions. Unless you're the CFO, Apple wants you to focus on your work, not on your P&L.

In *Steve Jobs*, Walter Isaacson's excellent biography of the Apple founder and CEO, there is a great story illustrating the value of focus.[2] Steve had just recently returned to Apple, and he was shocked to find how many different products the company was making. After a series of scathing meetings, Steve cut 70 percent of the company's product line. At one meeting, he drew a simple quadrant chart. He labeled the quadrants "consumer," "pro," "desktop," and "portable." He told his managers that he wanted "four great products, one for each quadrant," writes Isaacson.

Many of the managers were furious. But from Steve's perspective, he had just empowered them to focus on creating a small number of truly great products.

The success of Apple proves that simplicity, directness, focus, and accountability are critical qualities in a culture of innovation. Are those four qualities present in your organization?

Notes

1. Hunter Muller, *On Top of the Cloud: How CIOs Leverage New Technologies to Drive Change and Build Value Across the Enterprise* (Hoboken, NJ: John Wiley & Sons, 2012).

2. Walter Isaacson, *Steve Jobs* (New York: Simon & Schuster, 2011).

Chapter 3

Leveraging Multiple Skill Sets

In *The Innovator's DNA*, authors Jeff Dyer, Hal Gregersen, and Clayton M. Christensen list five "discovery skills" of disruptive innovators.[1] The five skills are associating, questioning, observing, networking, and experimenting.

It is interesting to note that none of those skills involves any special forms of technical expertise, experience, or even intelligence. Essentially, the critical skills listed in *The Innovator's DNA* are social skills. The authors seem to be saying that communication and interaction are fundamental parts of the modern innovation process. The authors write that "innovators are consummate questioners who show a passion for inquiry. Their queries frequently challenge the status quo."

Moreover, successful innovators act with courage. "First, they actively desire to change the status quo," according to the authors. "Second, they regularly take smart risks to make that change happen."

The authors found that innovative CEOs "spend 50 percent more time on discovery activities (questioning, observing, networking and experimenting) than CEOs with no innovation track record."

Innovative CEOs and entrepreneurs actually walk the talk. They are not just instructing the people around them to be more innovative; they are doing it themselves.

From my perspective, the takeaway is that innovation requires a combination of soft skills and hard skills, and a blending of multiple processes across several disciplines.

Networking and Connecting

In today's highly digitized global economy, innovation is often less about inventing, and more about networking and connecting. An innovative product does not necessarily create something from scratch; instead, it links two things that no one else linked before. Of the five discovery skills listed in *The Innovator's DNA*, associating comes first. As the book's authors note, Albert Einstein referred to creative thinking as "combinatorial play." It is hard to disagree with Einstein, a genius who loved to tinker with other people's ideas—and quite often raised them to a higher level.

In this book, we will look at various ways in which innovation leaders connect ideas, connect innovators with other innovators, and connect ideas with users. All of those activities raise the level of innovation, and keep the process going. Innovation rarely happens in isolation. The image of the lone scientist is largely mythic and does not represent the true nature of modern innovation, which tends to happen in groups, or is the result of group efforts.

Overcoming Obstacles to Innovation

Let us face it: Innovating is not easy. The life of an innovator can be hard, and the life of an innovation leader can be even harder. In an incredibly useful book, *Thinking, Fast and Slow*, Nobel laureate Daniel Kahneman examines the obstacles we face whenever we try to change the status quo.[2] Here's a quote from the book that sums up the way all animals—not just human beings—fear any type of change:

> *To survive in a frequently dangerous world, an organism should react cautiously to a novel stimulus, with withdrawal and fear. Survival prospects are poor for an animal that is not suspicious of novelty.*

I do not think you can state the problem more clearly than Kahneman does in his book. The good news, however, is that the fear fades after you realize that the new thing, whatever it is, is not actually dangerous. That is where the hope lies. That we can overcome fear when we realize that it is not necessary removes the excuse to stick with the status quo merely because it is the path of least resistance.

The key to overcoming fear is repeated exposure to the new stimulus. The more you see that it is not harmful, the less afraid you become. Pretty soon, you are not afraid of it at all—it has become the new normal.

From my perspective, that means that part of your role as a leader of innovation is exposing people to new ideas, new technologies, and new processes as often as possible.

In other words, make the experience of novelty part of everyone's routine. When innovation is just another part of the job, people are less likely to resist it.

Two Types of Thinking

As the title of Kahneman's book implies, human beings tend to think in two types of ways. One of those types is what Kahneman calls "fast thinking," or "System 1." That's the kind of thinking you do that's automatic, virtually subconscious, and almost always biased around your existing beliefs. It is intuitive, it feels natural, and as its name suggests, it happens very rapidly.

Then there's "slow thinking," which he also calls "System 2." That's the kind of thinking you do after the crisis is averted or the danger has passed. It is deliberative, it takes time, and it allows a more thorough examination of the facts than its faster counterpart.

I mention Kahneman's concepts because they are useful for understanding the obstacles that often prevent innovation from moving forward. By definition, innovation is something new. But as Kahneman reminds us, new things tend to frighten us. We respond with fast thinking, and because of our ingrained biases, we often reach the wrong conclusion.

When we are in the innovation mode—or when we're responsible for leading innovation strategy—we're going to rely on slow thinking to get the job done. But that means that we've got to train ourselves and train the people around us to recognize the differences between System 1 and System 2.

Our fast thinking processes will tend to reject anything that's new, unfamiliar, or strange. We have got to ramp up our slow thinking" abilities if we want to succeed at innovating.

Overcoming Habits

If you have not already read *The Power of Habit: Why We Do What We Do in Life and Business* by *New York Times* investigative reporter Charles Duhigg, I strongly urge you to buy, borrow, or download a copy.[3] It is a fast read, and it will give you a highly useful overview of the major obstacle standing between the status quo and innovation.

Duhigg describes the process by which habits are acquired and reinforced. More important, though, he writes about the ways for discarding old habits and replacing them with new ones.

"Habits can be changed, if we understand how they work," writes Duhigg. Habits begin as rational, deliberate choices. Over time, these choices harden into automatic, unconscious responses. It's almost as if they become hardwired into the operating systems of our brains. Some habits are helpful, and some are harmful.

Duhigg writes that he became interested in the power of habit when he was a reporter in Baghdad. The U.S. military, he explains, is "one of the biggest habit-formation experiments in history."

He describes a situation in which a U.S. Army major had accomplished something that had seemed impossible: He stopped a series of deadly riots in the plazas of a small city, Kufa.

The major knew he had a serious problem on his hands. One of the first things he did was review all the information he had available. He studied videos of the riots, looking for patterns in the behavior of the rioters. After carefully analyzing the images, he noticed a pattern and devised a solution to counter it. Here is Duhigg's description of the major's solution:

> *When the major met with Kufa's mayor, he made an odd request: Could they keep food vendors out of the plazas? Sure, the mayor said. A few weeks later, a small crowd gathered near the Masjid al-Kufa, or Great Mosque of Kufa. Throughout the afternoon, it grew in size. Some people began chanting angry slogans. . . . At dusk, the crowd started getting restless and hungry. People looked for the kebob sellers normally filling the plaza, but there were none to be found. The spectators left. The chanters became dispirited. By 8 p.m., everyone was gone.*
>
> *The major had observed and identified the key habit that had made the riots possible. Then he took action to break the habit. By breaking that habit, he stopped the riots.*

Fortunately, most of us will not be required to operate under similarly dangerous conditions. But think about your organization and see if you can identify the habits that are preventing or impeding innovation. Then think about ways of breaking those habits.

Breaking Through and Moving Forward

Unlike the major, the habits we are trying to break do not lead to riots. From a business perspective, however, habits can be stubborn enemies—especially when they prevent us from achieving our goals as leaders of innovation.

I found a treasure trove of useful insight and advice in *Conceptual Blockbusting: A Guide to Better Ideas* by James. L. Adams.[4] It is a genuinely excellent book, and several of the CIOs we interviewed for this book recommended it. In the book, Adams notes that "habits are often inconsistent with creativity. Creativity implies deviance from past procedure. . . . Habits often destroy creative ideas before they can see the light of day."

Solving problems often requires inventing new procedures and breaking old habits. But breaking habits is hard work, and it requires a process. As you might suspect, the process of breaking habits is not intuitive—if it were, everyone could do it.

Adams describes the mental blocks that make it difficult to devise new solutions for old problems. He lists six perceptual blocks "that prevent the problem-solver from clearly perceiving the problem itself or the information needed to solve the problem." Those six blocks are:

1. Detecting what you expect—stereotyping

2. Difficulty in isolating the problem

3. Tendency to delimit the problem area poorly

4. Inability to see the problem from various viewpoints

5. Saturation

6. Failure to utilize all sensory inputs

My purpose in including Adams's list of perceptual blocks isn't to provide you with a detailed roadmap for becoming a better problem solver by overcoming bad habits—my intention is to show you that it is possible to look at problem solving as a process, break it into several component parts, and tackle the various parts in a methodical manner.

The reason it is important to have a process is simple: Not all of us are Steve Jobs. Steve could apparently see problems and visualize solutions intuitively. He was a natural problem solver, and his solutions were often brilliant. Most of us, however, will have to rely on some kind of process or method to inspire creativity in ourselves and in the people around us. Hopefully this book is helping you move closer to developing or adopting the processes you will need to achieve your goals as a leader of innovation.

Professor of Innovation

I was recently introduced to Bruce Bachenheimer, clinical professor of management at Pace University's Lubin School of Business and director of the university's Entrepreneurship Lab. I think it is fair to say that Bruce lives and breathes innovation and entrepreneurship. A serial entrepreneur himself, Bruce is an expert on the important role that innovation plays in business growth.

In a lengthy interview, Bruce outlined some of the reasons he's passionate about innovation and entrepreneurship. Here's a summary of what he said:

As Thomas Friedman says, the world is flat. Countries compete on a much more equal basis than in the past. On a national level, the only sustainable competitive advantages come from innovation.

Competing on the basis of low labor costs is a temporary strategy. It's a race to the bottom and it won't keep you competitive in the long run. Nations with high standards of living, low unemployment, trade surpluses, and general prosperity tend to compete on innovation.

For a while, it seemed like Japan's strategy of competing on the basis of manufacturing efficiency was a winning strategy, but the gains they achieved disappeared as competition drove down prices, which benefited consumers, not manufacturers. It was a temporary victory, and now they've been in a recession for nearly two decades.

If you look at countries that are leaders in innovation—the U.S., Australia, New Zealand, Israel, and the countries in northern Europe—you see high levels of education and high levels of entrepreneurship. In Japan, for example, the culture and regulatory system make it very difficult for entrepreneurs to succeed. If you are an entrepreneur in Japan, you face a lot of barriers. As a society, Japan is very intolerant of failure. That fear of failure stops people from taking risks, and you need to take risks to succeed as an entrepreneur.

On the other hand, countries like the U.S. and Israel are much more tolerant of failure—especially when you fail on someone else's dime. Failure isn't exactly a badge of honor, but it's not a death sentence either. In the U.S., when someone's business fails, people are likely to say, "That guy really learned a lesson. He sure won't make that mistake again." People in entrepreneurial cultures tend to see failure as a learning experience.

Company cultures have a similar impact on innovation. Companies that encourage innovation and tolerate a certain amount of failure are more likely to be the serial innovators.

And it's important to remember that innovation does not have to be about technology. We all tend to think of Dell as a tech company, but Michael Dell's greatest innovations were selling PCs direct to consumers and mass customization. Neither of those innovations required advanced technologies; Dell used existing technology to do a great job of marketing and selling its products.

Same thing holds true for Facebook. Most of the technology had already been pioneered by Friendster,

MySpace, and other social networking platforms. Mark Zuckerberg's innovation was creating something that everyone could use.

I love how Bruce puts innovation and entrepreneurship into context, and show us the impact of innovation on multiple levels. Bruce also advises his students to think like innovative entrepreneurs when envisioning their career paths. In today's rapidly evolving and ever-changing economy, I think that is excellent advice for all of us.

Leveraging the Cloud and Thriving on Innovation

I had a great conversation recently with John Engates, the chief technology officer at Rackspace. John is a genuinely brilliant guy, and in our conversation he reminded me why the cloud has become such an important piece of innovation strategy.

First, some background on John: He joined Rackspace in August 2000, just a year after the company was founded, as vice president of operations, managing the data center operations and customer service teams. Two years later, when Rackspace decided to add new services for larger enterprise customers, John created and helped develop the Intensive Hosting business unit.

John plays an active role in the evolution and evangelism of Rackspace's cloud computing strategy and cloud products. He meets frequently with customers to hear about their needs and concerns, and to discuss Rackspace's vision for the future of cloud computing. He's also become an internationally recognized cloud computing expert and a sought-after speaker at technology conferences, including CA World, the Goldman Sachs Techtonics Conference, and Cloud Expo.

In our conversation, I asked him to explain the relationship between the cloud and innovation. Here's a brief summary of what he said:

> *Innovation is about trying things and oftentimes failing. Failure is a part of innovation. You don't know what will work until you try some things, and cloud computing lowers the barrier significantly to trying things and allowing things to fail. In the old world, the CIO would have to allocate hardware and resources in the spots that he thought had the best chance of winning. He would place his bets carefully because he only had so much resource to go around.*
>
> *With cloud computing, the resources are much more elastic and much more unlimited in the sense that you can try a lot of things all at once and you can fail at a few things and there really isn't any huge cost to failure. You're not stuck with equipment. You haven't built a data center. Haven't invested hundreds of hours in building out equipment. You can really fail very quickly. You're planting lots of seeds, knowing that some will grow and some won't.*

The cloud, says, John, allow you to avoid placing large bets on projects that might not deliver the return on investment you wanted. With the cloud, you can spread your bets. If a project works, you scale it up. If it doesn't, you shut it down. In either case, you haven't invested millions in new infrastructure. From my perspective, that's the power of the cloud.

I also asked John how the cloud could help CIOs explore and experiment the growing universe of advanced data analytics. Here's part of his reply:

Analytics are important today because we've got more data flowing than ever before. We've got transactional data, financial data, marketing data, social media data. We need analytics to make sense of all that data. We're all trying to find the needle in the haystack.

This is an area where the cloud and hosting really shine. Many analytics projects have a short life span. The technology is quite new and continually evolving. People are learning and experimenting with new platforms for high-speed analytics. Every week, someone introduces a new solution for handling big data.

The cloud allows you to spin up analytics projects very quickly, without making a huge investment. What we are discovering, however, is that new types of expertise are required to manage those types of projects. At Rackspace, we're working on ways to provide both the infrastructure and the expertise needed to leverage the potential of analytics and get the most out of it.

John also reminded me that Rackspace's cloud business began as a test product, became a subsidiary, and was folded back into the company core. So in a very real sense,

Rackspace is thriving on its own innovation. I think there are lots of great lessons here, and I look forward to hearing more from John and his team in the future.

Notes

1. Jeff Dyer, Hal Gregersen, and Clayton M. Christensen, *The Innovator's DNA: Mastering the Five Skills of Disruptive Innovators* (Boston: Harvard Business Review Press, 2011).

2. Daniel Kahneman, *Thinking, Fast and Slow* (New York: Farrar, Straus and Giroux, 2011).

3. Charles Duhigg, *The Power of Habit: Why We Do What We Do in Life and Business* (New York: Random House, 2012).

4. James L. Adams, *Conceptual Blockbusting: A Guide to Better Ideas* (New York: Basic Books, 2001).

Chapter 4

Accelerating Innovation

Thaddeus Arroyo, the CIO at AT&T, is a true visionary and IT leader. Thaddeus graciously shared his perspectives with the HMG Strategy team in a wide-ranging conversation about technology, innovation and business transformation. Thaddeus makes a strong case for IT leadership in a rapidly changing world. Here are edited highlights of his deep understanding and insight, gleaned from our conversation:

Information technology executives and professionals don't have to be told about the relationship between innovation and technology. They already know you can't have one without the other. They also know innovation is essential to business growth, and that it's been that way for a long time.

Today we're seeing a dramatic increase in the speed at which innovation occurs. Rapid shifts in technology are changing the way business does business. In this still-emerging and increasingly interconnected landscape, converging technologies are creating new opportunities at a pace that would have been inconceivable in the past.

What are the enablers of this new era of rapid transformation? Here are some examples: Advances in powerful mobile computing devices; connections to fast and ubiquitous networks; and services in a robust cloud infrastructure.

Those enablers currently allow companies to accomplish things that would have been hard to imagine a few years ago. The impact of those enablers will be felt for years to come.

When we talk about the "connected landscape," we're really talking about the convergence of technologies; the expanding, and ever more mobile, ubiquitous network that connects everything; and the rise of a mobilized society in which the distance from intent to action is shortened.

We're talking about new collaboration capabilities that move us from a "talk to me" culture to a "show me" culture; the rise of the cloud, shifting everything to shared infrastructure and allowing the emergence of smart objects and smarter interactions; and finally, changes in software are driving a proliferation of new applications, empowered by a common language of application programmer interfaces (APIs) that enables better integration.

It makes perfect sense to me that Thaddeus sees "the network" as a foundational element of the new IT landscape. I really like how he describes the network's role relative to the technologies that it supports and enables. Here are his words:

A smart, omnipresent network is empowering devices with the contextual and relevant data that people and companies need to interact more effectively with the world.

Right now, we are surrounded by network access points—macro, micro, pico, Wi-Fi—and we move between them without knowing it.

In the future, the network will become even more ubiquitous, disappearing from our consciousness as we interact with content and devices. Movement between these networks becomes more seamless.

How businesses make use of this smart, invisible network will define companies' offerings and successes for years to come.

Today, the rise of this ubiquitous network is driving a whole new Internet experience—the "Internet of Things," as the tech industry calls it.

The proliferation of people and things *connected to the Internet continues to swell. This is opening doors to endless opportunities in the way we innovate and capitalize.*

Today, 1.7 billion people connect to the Internet; that is forecast to expand to 4.7 billion users by 2020. But the Internet doesn't just connect users. In 2008, the number of devices connected to the Internet exceeded the number of people living on the planet. In 2010, we added 5.5 billion additional devices, to reach 12.5 billion device connections. By 2020, we'll have 50 billion device connections—nearly 10 times the number of users.

From his perspective, the connected world isn't just smartphones and tablets—it's a mash-up of connected devices: Sensors that make up the smart utility grid, smart factory automation devices, even the pill bottles that people reach for every day.

As Thaddeus points out, the traffic generated by machine-to-machine connections is expected to grow 2,200 percent by 2016. Consider the implications for a wireless world where everything—every *thing*—is connected! I particularly like the way Thaddeus sees a world that is expanding and shrinking at the same time. Here is his description of that new world:

> *Mobility is shortening the distance between intent and action. Today, we no longer have to drive to a physical location to complete errands . . . we're just as likely to use smart phones on the go—in stores, restaurants, on public transportation—as we are at home or work.*
>
> *In fact, 31 percent of American mobile Internet users use smartphones for* most *online activity.*
>
> *And this distance will get even shorter. Today, we take time from our busy days to go to the doctor's office for routine check-ups. Advances in mobile health care will make it possible in the future to collect this data remotely and store it in the cloud until the doctor needs it.*

Mobility capabilities will continue to evolve as society embraces smartphones and tablets. Tablets are changing how we read books and magazines, watch videos, and perform daily work activities. By the end of 2012, eMarketer forecasts 70 million tablet users in the United States. According to Thaddeus:

> *That's nearly 30 percent of Internet users in the country.*
>
> *Paralleling this user-based device evolution is the creation and rise of smart assets through the marriage of compute and connectivity.*

As we move towards a culture where everything is mobilized, we're seeing a dramatic shift in how people share information and experiences.

Social technologies are driving the flow of information faster and faster. Among those Americans who get news online today, 75 percent do so from e-mail or posts on social networking sites. And in another survey, more than half said they learned of breaking news via social media ahead of traditional news sources. 27 percent of Americans cite social media as their primary online news source, virtually the same number that cite online newspapers.

We're seeing the content consumer become the content creator, or co-collaborator. Anyone can build a website, or post a blog. On Facebook each day, 2.5 billion pieces of content—videos, posts, or photos—are exchanged by more than 1 billion active Facebook users.

As we look to the future, kids are growing up today as a connected generation. By 2020, this generation will make up 40% of the population in the U.S., Europe and BRIC countries [Brazil, Russia, India, China].

Cloud-based services and co-creation are embedded in their psyches. It's as natural to them as carrying a cell phone is most Americans today. Only, they've grown up plugged in 24 hours a day.

The ubiquitous broadband connectivity mentioned earlier lays the foundation for mobile access to the cloud. The cloud is transforming the way business does business, primarily because it enables a shift to shared infrastructure.

This means intelligence now moves from the device into the cloud, where anyone can access it, regardless of the device they're using. With the cloud, processing power can be delivered over the network. Apps and data can reside in the network, accessed on demand. Content and applications adapt to you—not the other way around.

The cloud is moving us towards a fluid future in which devices, services and the individual are dynamically linked. And in this fluid state, hardware disintegrates; software integrates.

That's the beauty of the cloud. It relieves devices of data constraints and applications of capability limitations by moving into a network-based infrastructure.

Where does this all lead? Today, companies have numerous opportunities to leverage technology for transformational change. There are many paths, and many challenges. But some of the steps are unambiguous: Organizations will increasingly use smarter devices, powered by a ubiquitous network, to elevate and transform their capabilities. They will leverage new collaboration tools to increase the speed and means for innovation within organizations. And they will re-examine their services and products in light of all the new paths to innovation.

Our conversation with Thaddeus closed on a high note and a clear vision of a bright future:

Every industry stands to benefit from the opportunities generated by today's technology advances. The convergence of mobility with innovations in the cloud, applications and devices, powered by a fast, pervasive digital network will transform lives and industries.

Now is the time to leverage advances in technology to drive innovation. It starts with companies reshaping organizations, reinventing offerings, and anticipating change. For change, as we know, is the only thing that remains constant.

In the Modern Enterprise, IT Is the Backbone of Innovation

I had a wonderful conversation with N S Bala recently, and I am delighted to share his opinions and insights with you in this section of the book.

First, some background: Bala is senior vice president of the Manufacturing and High-Tech Industry Strategic Business Unit of Wipro Technologies. The division employs 9,000 people and contributes over 19 percent of the global revenues of Wipro Technologies.

Over the years, Bala has restructured the business unit to deepen its focus on specific subindustry segments, building a strong customer advisory capability and offering integrated services across business process, applications, and infrastructure. He has also been instrumental in driving innovation in delivery through models such as the Factory Model and Center for Integrated Global Management of Applications (Cigma), which won Wipro the NASSCOM Innovation Award and was featured in the book *Bangalore Tiger* by Steve Hamm.

Bala's pioneering use of Toyota Production Systems principles in application and software development was developed into a case study by the Harvard Business School and is now taught to MBA candidates.

From Bala's perspective, successful innovation depends on a blend of scale and agility. IT is a key player in innovation strategy because it provides the "backbone" that enables and supports all of the various processes required for surfacing ideas, identifying and differentiating winning ideas, and moving those winning ideas swiftly into production.

"Volatility is here to stay," says Bala. "Volatility in markets is the new normal. Your company's ability to respond quickly to changes in markets is absolutely crucial for long-term success. So you have to be very agile."

Despite widespread agreement that agility and innovation are important, many companies still find it difficult to embrace the cultural changes that are fundamental to innovation. Many companies are encumbered by traditional management hierarchies that try to control innovation from the top down. These companies tend to rely on "innovation labs," special teams, or outside consultants to generate innovation. But those top-down approaches to innovation seem increasingly out of touch with the realities of modern global competition.

"The best ideas often come from the edge of the company, rather than from its core," says Bala. "So you need the ability to gather ideas from the edge and refine them into new products and services that you can bring to market. Your ability to accomplish this swiftly is critical, because today's markets move very rapidly."

When Bala speaks about "edge," he includes the company's employees, partners, and customers. In other words, you should expect one-third of innovation to come from within the company and two-thirds to come from outside the company.

This perspective might seem counterintuitive, but it's very sensible, especially when you consider it in the light of recent findings in experimental neuroscience: Innovative ideas generally occur while you are focusing on something else.

The best ideas often arise unexpectedly. You can't really predict the time or place. What you can and should do, however, is create a robust process for capturing those ideas whenever and wherever they arise.

That is where the IT backbone becomes a genuine competitive advantage; it provides a platform and a repeatable process for continuous innovation. When you do something over and over, it becomes your culture. A company that supports a culture of innovation is going to be more agile—and therefore more competitive—than a company that relies on a top-down innovation strategy.

Underlying Principles of Innovation

What is the best way to create a culture of innovation in a modern enterprise? In *Macrowikinomics: New Solutions for a Connected Planet*, Don Tapscott and Anthony D. Williams lay down five principles for what they describe as a new "age of networked intelligence."[1] A thorough reading of their book convinced me that those five principles can also be applied to cultures of innovation. The five principles are:

1. Collaboration

2. Openness

3. Sharing

4. Integrity

5. Interdependence

Take a moment to reflect on your organization. Are those principles in place, and are they being followed by the people within the organization? Are managers and executives providing leadership that promotes and reinforces those principles?

Following those principles does not merely make the organization a better place to work. The principles outlined in *Macrowikinomics* are critical to the survival and success of the organization. The authors note that

we are seeing how the age of networked intelligence renders conventional approaches to value creation insufficient, and in some cases, completely inappropriate. Collaborative innovation, for example, is killing the old, hardwired "plan and push" mentality taught in business schools.

Commenting of their years of research, the authors observe that the "common thread . . . is the growing realization that the collective knowledge, capability, and resource embodied within broad horizontal networks of participants can accomplish more than one organization or one individual can acting alone."

A Practical Taxonomy of Innovation

In *Dealing with Darwin: How Great Companies Innovate at Every Phase of Their Evolution*, respected business guru Geoffrey A. Moore outlines specific types or "vectors" of innovation that take place within four categories or "zones" of business strategy.[2] According to Moore, a company's current business strategy should determine the way in which it approaches innovation. Here is my ultraquick overview of the taxonomy offered in *Dealing with Darwin*:

- If your company is in the Product Leadership Zone, focus on Disruptive Innovation, Application Innovation, Product Innovation, or Platform Innovation.

- If your company is in the Customer Intimacy Zone, focus on Line-Extension Innovation, Enhancement Innovation, Marketing Innovation, or Experiential Innovation.

- If your company is in the Operational Excellence Zone, focus on Value-Engineering Innovation, Integration Innovation, Process Innovation, or Value-Migration Innovation.

- If your company is in the Category Renewal Zone, focus on Organic Innovation or Acquisition Innovation.

If you have not already read *Dealing with Darwin*, I urge you to pick up a copy so you can examine Moore's innovation taxonomy in greater detail. From my perspective, the main takeaways are:

- Innovation is a critical element of business strategy.

- Innovation is a continuous process that includes multiple subprocesses; the proper selection of processes depends on your company's current business strategy.

- Innovation requires a disciplined and scientific approach.

"The single more important act of strategic leadership is to select the innovation vector upon which your company will develop its sustainable competitive advantage—its core," writes Moore.

It is hard to disagree with that advice, and it supports my growing belief that innovation should not be approached haphazardly or informally. If you believe that innovation is critical to success, then it makes sense to develop a formal innovation strategy.

The Mouse in the Maze

Much has been written about Steve Jobs's unique and highly secretive approach to innovation and business success. I believe that much of Steve's public persona was a studied effort in misdirection and that in truth, his approach to business was fairly normal for an entrepreneur.

Steve's approach to innovation seems very different from that of his archrival, Bill Gates. For Steve, innovation was not a direct line; there were lots of twists and turns on the path to success. My hunch is that for Steve and other visionary entrepreneurs, innovation is less like sitting under a tree and waiting for inspiration than it is like navigating a tortuous maze or a labyrinth.

Malcolm Gladwell, the author of bestselling books such as *The Tipping Point*, *Blink*, and *Outliers*, wrote an absolutely fascinating article for the May 16, 2011, edition of the *New Yorker*, entitled "Creation Myth: Xerox PARC, Apple, and the Truth About Innovation."[3]

In the article, Gladwell describes a 1979 visit by Steve to PARC, the legendary research center of Xerox Corporation. Back in those days, Xerox was on top of the world. Apple was a hot tech firm, but it was tiny by comparison. According to one of the PARC scientists cited by Gladwell, Steve seemed "rambunctious."

Steve's tour of PARC included a demonstration of a Xerox Alto, the company's personal computer. Two things impressed Steve about the Xerox PC: The engineer running the demo used a device he called a "mouse" to move a cursor around on the PC's screen, and he could open pop-up menus on the screen by clicking on icons with the mouse.

The common myth is that Steve "stole" the ideas for the mouse and the icons from Xerox PARC and incorporated them into the Macintosh. Gladwell rightly identifies two problems with that myth: First, PARC had borrowed the idea for its mouse from Douglas Engelbart, a computer scientist at the nearby Stanford Research Institute whose mouse was a bulky wooden shell with two metal wheels. Second, when you clicked on an icon on the screen of your Macintosh, you did not merely open a menu—you opened a program. That feature was inspired by Steve's idea that users should be able to manipulate programs directly.

It is also important to note that when Steve hired an outside design firm to create a mouse for Apple, he specifically told them that it had to cost less than $15 to manufacture and had to be durable enough to last for years—unlike the Xerox mouse, which cost several hundred dollars to construct and broke easily.

So the notion that Steve walked into PARC and somehow walked out with clear visions in his mind of a series of incredibly innovative products that would change the world is pure fiction.

"If you lined up Engelbart's mouse, Xerox's mouse, and Apple's mouse, you would not see the serial reproduction of an object. You would see the evolution of a concept," writes Gladwell.

I recommend reading Gladwell's article, which you can download from the *New Yorker* digital archive. According to

Gladwell, the evolution of technology often takes a circuitous path. Another example he cites is the use of complex digital technologies in modern combat. The idea of applying high technology to warfare is credited to a group of senior military leaders of the Soviet Union. The United States developed the actual systems in the 1970s, and Israel used similar systems in its decisive victory over the Syrian Air Force in 1982.

"In the history of the mouse, Engelbart was the Soviet Union. He was the visionary, who saw the mouse before anyone else did," writes Gladwell. If Engelbart played the role of the Soviet Union in Gladwell's analogy, then Xerox was the United States and Apple was Israel.

In his article, Gladwell sees three distinct strands in the innovation process, each strand representing different sets of skills and circumstances. The first strand represents the visionary, the second represents the builder, and the third represents the marketer.

Managing Innovation Across the Enterprise

Talking about innovation is easy. The real challenge is managing and supporting innovation in a modern corporate environment.

Hunter Jones is the CIO at Houston-based Cameron, a leading provider of flow equipment products, systems, and services to worldwide oil, gas, and process industries. I had a great conversation with him recently, and we spoke mostly about the key role of IT in facilitating innovation across the enterprise. Here is a brief summary of what he told me:

Innovation is critical because you always want to be a step ahead. You're always looking over the next horizon and trying to figure out where you need to be. A large part of my role is helping the company prepare for the future.

The role of IT is providing innovation for the business. Sometimes that means helping the business decide where innovation can have the most impact. Some areas of the business can benefit more from innovation than others. Everyone can't be at the head of the class. That would be impractical.

In IT, we established innovation committees for our key business process areas—engineering, finance, sales, operations, supply chain, aftermarket, et cetera. Each committee is "sponsored" by an executive from a different part of the enterprise. That creates healthy levels of commitment, participation, and buy-in.

The committees present their ideas quarterly to my executive steering committee. That ensures that we're all on the same page in terms of priorities. The net result is that we bring innovation to the business more quickly, and with greater confidence.

Within the context of the innovation committees, IT serves as coach and facilitator to the business areas. The committees themselves form a practical framework for an enterprise-wide collaborative process that inspires trust.

Higher levels of trust help the enterprise to move forward with greater speed, agility, and confidence. Put all of that together and you have a competitive advantage.

The innovation process described by Hunter seems especially practical for large companies serving rapidly evolving global markets. One of the prime values of his approach is that its focus is more on the management of technology than on technology itself. As Hunter says, "It's about IT bringing innovation to the business."

Eight Action Steps for Driving Innovation

As discussed earlier, there is a clear tension between the need for achieving the highest possible level of operational excellence and a sustainable state of continuous innovation. Even in situations where the CIO's prime responsibility is safeguarding the company's IT assets, the general relationship between risk and reward holds true: Lower risk is associated with lower potential profit, and higher risk is associated with higher potential profit.

Good CIOs strive to balance operational excellence and innovation. I am beginning to think, however, that the truly great CIOs do not seek balance, at least not in the traditional sense of the word. Instead they seek a sort of dynamic equilibrium in which a blend of factors (market conditions, organizational capabilities, competitive strategy, available resources, timing, etc.) create a continually evolving range of options. They don't see things in black and white—they try to see the full continuum of choices and opportunities available at any particular moment.

My good friend Tom Fountain is a true IT thought leader and visionary. As many of you know, Tom has served as CIO at several major corporations, including Bunge and Honeywell. Tom has generously shared the basic template he uses when consulting with clients seeking practical innovation strategies that will succeed in today's hard-to-predict markets.

One of the takeaways I got from my conversations with Tom is the idea that innovation sits between vision and execution. It's part of a larger process or continuum that looks like this:

Vision → Innovation → Execution

According to Tom, the biggest challenge for leaders is connecting the dots between innovation and execution. If you can't get execution part right, the innovation part won't matter.

Tom uses a matrix like the one shown in Table 4.1 to illustrate why it is important to connect the innovation and execution parts of the process.

"The matrix helps you visualize each step of the innovation process, because you're going to innovate differently in different situations," says Tom. "For example, introducing a better feature in an existing market requires a different approach to

Table 4.1   Innovation and Execution

	Existing markets	New markets
New features		Most potential risks; Highest potential profit
Better features	Fewest potential risks; Lowest potential profit	

innovating than introducing the same feature in a new market, or introducing a radically new feature in a new market."

I think that Tom makes a great point, and one that is frequently overlooked. There is no one-size-fits-all approach to innovation. Your approach should vary with the circumstances.

That being said, Tom provided me with his list of eight action steps that will greatly improve your chances of bringing innovations to market successfully:

1. **Bring the need to the people who are innovating.** Innovation tends to take place in offices that are far from the front lines. Since the people on the front lines typically have firsthand knowledge of how customers perceive and use the company's products, make sure there's a way for transmitting that hands-on knowledge back to the people who are innovating. In other words, don't try to innovate in a vacuum.

2. **Lower the cost of risk.** Fail fast and fail cheaply. Make it easy for people to admit when a project isn't heading in the right direction. If you punish people for

failure, they'll keep working on a project even when they know it's the wrong solution.

3. **Provide the basic tools and broad access to knowledge.** This step builds on the first two action steps on the list. Make sure that innovators have access to information from a variety of sources, and provide them with some type of internal collaboration platform so they can share what they learn.

4. **Energize people about the impact of their projects.** Let people know that the innovation projects they're working on are important, relevant, and worth the effort. It's amazing how often this critical step is overlooked or neglected.

5. **Mix the generations.** Make sure that innovation teams include people from all parts of the company and at all stages of career development. Mix experienced people and less experienced people, veteran employees and new hires, accountants and marketers, and so on.

6. **Field the team, not just the product.** When a product is ready for field testing, bring the innovation team into the field to observe the tests. Let the people who worked on the project see how the market responds, how customers react, and how their ideas play out in the world outside.

7. **Create constructive envy.** Make sure that when an innovation is successful, you promote it within the company. Let the divisions and units know what the other divisions and units are doing. When division A sees division B

succeed through innovation, division A will be inspired to innovate and go beyond the achievements of division B.

8. **Encourage people to find, as opposed to build.** Not every innovation must be built from scratch. Some of the most valuable innovations arise from combining existing products or services in new ways that no one had thought of before. Encourage people to modify or repurpose existing solutions before building new ones from the ground up.

Notes

1. Don Tapscott and Anthony Williams, *Macrowikinomics: Rebooting Business and the World* (New York: Portfolio, 2010).

2. Geoffrey A. Moore, *Dealing with Darwin: How Great Companies Innovate at Every Phase of Their Evolution* (New York: Portfolio, 2005).

3. Malcolm Gladwell, *The Tipping Point: How Little Things Can Make a Big Difference* (New York: Back Bay Books, 2002); Malcolm Gladwell, *Blink: The Power of Thinking Without Thinking* (New York: Little, Brown, 2005); Malcolm Gladwell, *Outliers: The Story of Success* (New York: Little, Brown, 2008).

Chapter 5

Innovation Begins with Business Strategy

Kim Stevenson is vice president and CIO at Intel, a company whose name has become synonymous with innovation. I asked her recently if she believes that innovation is a top-down strategy or a bottom-up process. Here's a brief summary of her reply:

> *Strategy and process are not mutually exclusive. They coexist, and they both serve the same purpose: helping the company execute on its business plan. That's why I don't like it when people say that "IT is aligned with the business." That's a weak expression. IT is part of the business. IT is everywhere in the company, helping the business execute its strategy and achieve its objectives. When innovation is part of the business strategy, IT is right there, helping the company execute.*

I really appreciate Kim's frank response. From her perspective, the idea of separating strategy, execution, and IT does not make sense. IT is part of the company and it plays a crucial role in executing company strategy.

IT's role is not achieving alignment with the business—IT's role is helping the business achieve its objectives and accomplish its mission.

When innovation is required, IT supports that innovation. When pure execution is required, IT makes it happen. The relationship between IT and the business is both simple and powerful: Work together, get it done.

"The business creates the space for people to think creatively," says Kim. "The Intel culture has a high tolerance for risk. That's one of the reasons we are innovative. But our innovations are driven by our business plans. Our plans are strong, and that strength empowers us to innovate successfully."

If strong business plans are a prerequisite for successful innovation, I think it is fair to say that weak business plans would make it awfully difficult for a company to pursue an innovation strategy with any real hope of success.

Here is the net takeaway from my conversation with Kim: Innovation starts with business strategy—you cannot innovate in a vacuum. The idea of separating innovation, business strategy, and execution is a nonstarter, because they are truly inseparable and inextricably bound together in the modern enterprise.

The New Face of IT Executive Leadership

One of the reasons I love my job is because it offers me the opportunity to speak and engage with the world's smartest and most capable IT executives. In dozens of conversations over the past several months, two common themes have emerged:

1. Successful IT organizations reinvent themselves around mobile, social, and cloud computing.

2. Successful IT executives focus on leadership, innovation, and transformation strategies to keep their organizations relevant to the business.

Those are the big themes of modern IT. It is rare to hear anyone talking about gigabytes and servers these days. Most of the conversations involve business strategy.

That is a big shift in perspective, but the best IT executives have already made the leap. They are not fixating on technology—they are making substantive, meaningful contributions to the business. Often they are partnering, or exploring partnerships, with innovative companies such as Salesforce.com, Workday, IBM, VMware, and Box.

I spoke recently about this with Doug Schneider, vice president and chief technology officer, Canada at Manulife Financial Corp. Here is a brief summary of what Doug told me in our conversation:

Innovation isn't about moving from one class of server to another class of server. It's not about upgrading your disk drive so it runs faster. It's not about lowering per-gigabyte costs by 5 percent.

Maybe 10 years ago those were acceptable definitions of innovation. Today, you need to help the business achieve its goals. You need to help the business manage change.

I'm hard pressed to think of a situation in which IT isn't fundamental to the success of the business. The CIO or CTO should be a leader of change. You have to help the business use technology to get products and services to market quicker, to stay ahead of the competition. That's the role of IT in a modern organization. We're helping the business get to market faster.

I see the need for much tighter links between IT and marketing than ever before. I think that today's IT leaders need much deeper knowledge of markets.

IT leaders need to understand what markets want so they can help the business adopt new technologies and new capabilities that customers expect to see when they interact with you via the Web or their mobile devices.

That's the future of IT—understanding what the customer wants and helping the business adapt to the changing needs of its customers.

I genuinely believe that Doug has described the new face of IT executive leadership. In today's fast-changing global economy, the need for innovation and the need for leadership seem inseparable. If that is the case, it makes sense for IT to provide both.

Improvisational Skills Can Elevate Innovation Leadership Capabilities

Jim Tosone has an interesting career history. He was an IT leader at Pfizer for 30 years and served as head of the company's Healthcare Informatics Group. As he moved into management, a career coach suggested that he join Toastmasters to improve his communication skills and also join an improvisation group to enhance his collaboration and creativity skills. Here is Jim's story in his own words:

I was your stereotypical IT professional. I was introverted. I wanted to figure out everything myself and do everything myself. I didn't think communication was an important skill.

But when I moved into management, I had problems communicating with staff, peers, and internal clients. My experience in Toastmasters International and at the Second City Training Center (the world's leading organization for improvisation) changed my life. The people I worked with at Pfizer noticed the difference, and they asked me to conduct improv workshops for other managers.

I left Pfizer in 2010 and decided that my next career would not be health-care IT consulting but helping organizations enhance their creativity, collaboration, and communication skills using improvisation. In a sense, my new career was improvised.

The rest, as they say, is history. Jim is now a respected coach with major clients in many industries. We asked him to explain why improvisational skills are important for leaders of innovation. Here's a summary of his response:

Executives are well trained, both in college and on the job, to think critically. They're trained to spot flaws in an idea. They look for risks and hidden costs. They anticipate negative reactions from various stakeholders.

But they have less training in the art of possibility. One of the key concepts in improvisation is called "Yes and . . . ." What that means is when you are present-ed with an idea, you acknowledge the idea and you "accept" it.

Acceptance means a willingness to explore the idea, to find out what's good and right about the idea, and to build on or enhance it. Only after the idea has been fully explored do you go into critical-thinking mode.

The downside of the traditional approach, in which you go into critical-thinking mode first, is that thousands of good ideas with real possibility get strangled in the cradle.

We asked Jim to define improvisation and explain why innovation leaders should consider it an essential skill:

Improvisation is the art of making things up on the spur of the moment in real time. When you improvise, you respond to what's going on around you. You are hyperaware of your physical environment and, most important, the other people whom you're interacting with.

In the context of business innovation, which is about creating a product or service that is new and original, improvisation is a set of techniques for creating something with little or no preparation. Improvisation helps you respond rapidly.

We all know the pace of change in business is accelerating. We often do not have the time to develop elaborate plans. Increasingly, we need the ability to spot opportunities as they present themselves and to be comfortable with responding quickly.

Improvisational exercises help you become more comfortable dealing with rapid and unexpected change. If you watch an improv performance group doing a scene, you'll see that sometimes the rules of the game that underlie the scene change in some completely unforeseen way. The players have been trained to embrace the new situation and the possibilities it offers without fear or hesitation.

Executives always tell people that they need to think out of the box, become better team players, and do a better job of listening. But those are skills and behaviors that you need to learn, practice, and internalize. That's what improvisational exercises are designed to do—learn and practice those skills so that when you get into a real situation where you need them, you are comfortable and confident.

Some improvisational exercises involve using the idea of constraints to enhance traditional brainstorming activities. Jim explains how it works:

A major consumer products company brought me in because the executives wanted to brainstorm ideas on how they could accelerate the delivery of a major project. One of the exercises we did was called "ABC." The participants are asked to improvise a scene, but each line they speak has to begin with the next letter of the alphabet. So the first person starts by saying a line that begins with the letter "A," the next person says with a line that begins with the letter "B," and so on through the alphabet.

The exercise demonstrates how constraints can actually make you more creative. It works by distracting the logical, linear side of your brain, which then sets free the nonlogical, nonlinear side, allowing more creative ideas to emerge.

The group found that for each sequence of 26 ideas that they brainstormed, they surfaced 3 or 4 creative ones that would not have surfaced without the constraints. The constraints forced them to be more creative. For example, imagine you have to cut your budget by 10 percent. You can do that by trimming a few expenses here and there. But if you have to cut your budget by 40 percent, you have to get very creative. You have to start thinking about new and different ways of working and doing things that you wouldn't have considered if that constraint wasn't placed upon you.

Jim also explained how modern collaboration is different from traditional brainstorming.

They're different in a couple of important ways. Often what happens in brainstorming sessions is, while other people are tossing out ideas, you're not really listening because you're trying to come up with your own ideas. You're not fully engaged with them.

In improv-based collaboration, you listen to what other people are saying, acknowledge them, accept their ideas, and build on them. It's less about positions and advocacy and more about exploration and cocreation.

I really like how Jim makes the distinction between modern collaboration and traditional brainstorming. From my perspective, collaboration is an essential part of innovation, and collaboration requires many of the same skills involved in improvisation: the ability to listen carefully, work closely in small teams, and generate meaningful responses rapidly in a continually changing environment.

Blending Innovation and Operations

Tim Stanley is an independent consultant and former senior vice president of Enterprise Strategy + Cloud Innovation at Salesforce.com.

Before joining Salesforce.com, Tim was CIO and senior vice president of innovation, gaming, and technology at Harrah's Entertainment, another highly innovative company. Tim clearly understands innovation at the tactical and strategic levels. I spoke recently with Tim and asked him to describe the qualities required to become an innovation leader at a major enterprise. Here is a brief summary of what he told me:

First, you must be willing to look at things differently, challenge the status quo, and question "traditional" assumptions to effect change.

Second, you have to understand how the existing processes and systems work. You have to be a realist, and understand what's possible and what's practical. You also need to know what the enterprise can do, and what it can't (or won't) do without a catalyst for change.

Third, you need an "outside in" perspective—what I call the "orthogonal view." If not you or someone in your domain, it can often be someone from another industry who's done something analogous to what you're trying to accomplish. It's really helpful to look at the problem from a different perspective and with an out-of-the-box approach to solutions.

I really love the idea of the "orthogonal" perspective, because it suggests that you need a circle of people you can count on for good advice and honest counsel. I have been saying for years that what CIOs really need are strong networks of peers. As more companies look to their CIOs to find innovative, technology-based solutions for real-world business challenges, CIOs will need people they can trust to provide candid, useful feedback.

Tim's enlightened approach to innovation is highly valuable, both conceptually and practically. Following his logic, it seems clear to me that the "CIO innovation skill set" includes three distinct components or steps:

1. Seeing the "as is" state (i.e., the present).

2. Envisioning the "to be" state (i.e., the future).

3. Infusing the future vision with external insights and best practices from other industries.

The "hard part," says Tim, is "successfully blending innovation back into the operational part of the business." In other words, innovation needs context—it needs to be relevant in some way to the business strategy.

There is no doubt in my mind that Tim is a true innovation thought leader, and I genuinely look forward to our next conversation.

Innovating in the Battle Against Cancer

I had the pleasure of speaking with Jay Ferro recently. Jay is the CIO at the American Cancer Society, which will celebrate its hundredth birthday in 2013. Fighting cancer requires innovating on many fronts, including IT. Here's how Jay looks at it.

We hope this will be our last century. We're actively trying to put ourselves out of business.

Innovation is a strategic pillar of what we do. When you look at successful organizations, you see common threads. Innovation is one of those golden threads that we try to weave through everything we do. Innovation is part of our culture.

For example, our constituents are very different today compared to 10, 15, or 50 years ago. We're talking to several demographics. As a result, we need to be extremely flexible, extremely nimble. We have to meet our constituents on their turf and engage with them multiple ways. Whether you are a volunteer, a donor, a caregiver for someone who has cancer, a cancer patient or a survivor, or somebody who has lost someone to cancer—we have to be able to engage with you.

"Sending out mailers is still very effective with some segments of our constituency, but Gen Y and Millennials tend to engage differently. Social media and mobile are huge parts of what we're doing to engage with our younger demographic segments.

Like most CIOs, Jay is also responsible for driving down operational costs wherever possible. "Even while you're innovating, you still have to keep your eye on the ball. One of my goals is reducing our operating burden, so we can focus more resources on value-added things. We do that through using more cloud services, reducing complexity, and reducing redundancy. We're driving standardization and simplification and seeking economies of scale. The money we save is money that we can plow back into our mission."

Jay is quick to note that innovation isn't just an IT priority. "I report directly to our staff president and chief operating officer, and IT has a seat at the table with executive leadership. Innovation has to support the strategic mission of the organization. We're not doing innovation for innovation's sake. People donate to the American Cancer Society because they want to see cancer eradicated as a major public health problem."

That being said, nobody expects the society to remain unchanged over 100 years. "People expect us to be a nimble and adaptive organization," says Jay. "Relay For Life is a great example of innovation. It started in 1985 with a doctor in the Pacific Northwest, Dr. Gordy Klatt, circling a track for 24 hours to raise money to fight cancer."

Today, over 5,200 Relay For Life events across the United States raise more than $4 billion to save lives from cancer. In addition, the society licenses 20 nongovernmental organizations in other countries to hold Relay For Life events to battle cancer across the globe.

"It all started with somebody who had an innovative idea and a passion for what he wanted to do and a mission that he believed in," says Jay. "You go from one guy walking in circles for a day to millions of people supporting the cause. Now you can manage your Relay For Life team from a mobile app. You don't even have to go online. You can do everything—e-mail, Twitter, Facebook—from the app on your phone or tablet."

I really love how Jay and his team at the American Cancer Society leverage various new technologies to fight a critical battle on behalf of all humanity. Jay's efforts provide important lessons for all of us to learn.

Focusing on Value Creation, Improved Margins, and Staying Ahead of the Trend Curve

When you ask Tony Leng for his take on the current state of IT leadership, he always delivers. Tony is a top executive recruiter in the San Francisco area, and he really has his finger on the pulse of today's IT industry.

I spoke with him about the trends that will have the most impact on CIOs and senior IT leaders in the coming months. I asked him which trends are around the corner and over the horizon. Here is a brief summary of what he told me:

> *Obviously, the ongoing trends are cloud, mobile, and social computing—CloMoSo. But the major underlying trend is value creation. That's where CIOs need to focus—on helping their companies develop new markets, new customers, and new products. CIOs need to help their companies improve margins, get more from existing customers, and hit*

their targets more quickly. Today, it's really all about speed and margins.

From a technology perspective, the hottest trends are big data and the consumerization of IT. The consumerization trend has two subtrends: greater user empowerment and "gamification," which is the use of gamelike applications to engage with audiences more effectively than ever before.

User empowerment is rapidly extending beyond BYOD (bring your own device) to BYOA (bring your own application). That's a shift that CIOs will need to embrace and manage. CIOs will have to make sure that IT is a shaper, and not an obstacle, as these newer trends take hold.

Here in the Bay Area, we have many companies that understand these trends and are taking advantage of them to grow. Two of the most obvious examples are Facebook and Salesforce.com. Companies such as Okta, Workday, and Box are also leveraging the trends I mentioned, and are really providing great products.

Many of the health-care companies in our region are also making tremendous strides and achieving amazing results through their understanding of these key trends.

So my advice to CIOs is this: Keep your eyes on cloud, mobile, and social computing. Learn all you can about big data and analytics. Be aware of the multiple impacts of IT consumerization, and don't be surprised by the demand for gamelike apps in all kinds of scenarios.

This is an exciting time to be in IT, but you'll need to move fast if you want to be a leader.

That is truly valuable insight from a guy who genuinely knows the industry. I'm glad that he cited Okta, Workday, and Box as innovation leaders in the rapidly expanding universe of cloud, mobile, and social. To that list, I would add ServiceNow, Good Technology, NetSuite, IBM, and HP.

Escaping the Pull of the Past

Ralph Loura, the CIO at Clorox, sees IT leaders playing a fundamental role in driving innovation, even at companies that aren't perceived as technology-based organizations.

From Ralph's perspective, the days in which IT leaders were expected to focus primarily on transactional enterprise systems and process automation are largely over.

"That wasn't a bad thing," says Ralph. "As a result of those efforts, many organizations are much more efficient than ever before. As IT leaders, however, we need to escape the pull of the past."

In previous decades, transformational IT projects were performed "deep in the boiler room." In today's rapid-fire economy, IT leaders are expected to work more closely with the customer-facing parts of the business.

"Almost every major market and industry vertical has been disrupted in some significant way by recent technology trends," says Ralph. "IT will play an integral role in sorting out all of those newer technologies and helping businesses make the most of them."

Product development processes that used to cost millions of dollars and take months or even years to complete can now be accomplished in weeks by using combinations of cloud, social, and mobile technologies. In the consumer packaged goods industry, for example, companies are leveraging social media to accelerate new product development and gather incredibly useful insights from potential customers.

"In the past, when we needed deep insights on a product, we had to do extensive product testing. When we had a product innovation, we had to make prototypes, sit a bunch of people in a room behind a one-way glass, show them the new product, ask questions, take notes, observe their behavior, and gather information. And we'd have to repeat that process all over the country, for various geographic and demographic segments of the market," says Ralph.

"Today, companies can get the information they need with a collaborative portal. We can seek ideas, input, and feedback. We can dramatically reduce the innovation cycle time and get new products to market much faster. It's a radically different approach than what we were doing in the past."

In today's interconnected and socialized world, the CIO is the prime enabler of collaboration and cocreation. "More and more value is being created through collaboration. Part of the CIO's new role is helping the company bring all of those perspectives together and to help the company create new products and services that are genuinely interesting, different, and valuable."

With an end-to-end view of company processes, the CIO is uniquely positioned to gather insight from disparate parts of the organization. "IT sits at the juncture point of enterprise," says Ralph. "We are a window into every function and area of the corporation. From our position, we can bring forward ideas from every part of the enterprise. We can connect people, and we can create models and processes for moving their ideas through the stages of innovation and development."

I really like how Ralph is helping us redefine the CIO's portfolio. In the past, the CIO was mostly a steward of IT assets. Today, the CIO is also seen as a focal point of innovation.

My key takeaway from our conversation is that CIOs should be ready to provide executive leadership and ongoing support for enterprise collaboration strategies. Those strategies will be long term. In other words, innovation is not a trend, it's is the new normal.

My other takeaway is that CIOs should be outspoken advocates for innovation. They should take active, visible, high-level roles in surfacing the best ideas from across the enterprise and bringing those ideas to the C-suite.

Not every company will have the same approach to innovation. Some will stick to the older R&D model, and some will opt for more collaborative models. Some will form alliances with smaller and more agile companies to develop new ideas outside the traditional corporate hierarchy. And some will invent entirely new strategies and processes for enabling continuous innovation.

One thing seems certain: The CIO has a major role to play in supporting, enabling, and driving innovation. It's an important role, and from my perspective, it represents a significant elevation in responsibility.

Chapter 6

Evolving Relationships Across the C-Suite

When I met recently with the CIO Executive Leadership Alliance in New York City, one of the speakers was Linda Ban, Global CIO Study Program director from IBM. Linda presented on the implications paper from the IBM Institute of Business Value, which analyzed the interviews from 3,200-plus CIOs and 1,700-plus chief marketing officers (CMOs) on the changing relationship between these two executives.

Surprisingly, "while CMOs feel underprepared to manage the impact of market factor changes, CIOs are poised to help in a number of areas." Linda elaborated by showing how many new demands are being placed on marketing, such as social media, channel and device choices, and data explosion, all of which happen to be areas of IT expertise. Likewise, "CIO projects for improving organizational competitiveness correlate to the CMO's technology focus areas." The top three overlap areas include: business intelligence and analytics, social networking, and mobility solutions. With these common goals and intersecting opportunities at your company, are the CMO and CIO acquaintances or allies?

"The CIOs' opportunity to drive value extends beyond technology solutions, and includes the responsibility of overall data management, privacy, and compliance. There are gaps in the CMOs' understanding of the importance of data management, governance, and risk management," says Linda. Given the knowledge and strengths of IT, the CIO has an incredible opportunity to educate the business, which can drive business value, or at a minimum prevent catastrophic loss through proper security and controls.

The opportunity here is not just a one-way street with only IT offering up knowledge and solutions. A primary area in which many CIOs struggle is collaboration, both internal and external. Here is an area where marketing can offer years of experience from collaborating and owning the relationship with the customer.

To go from acquaintance to ally will take time. For you, part of this journey may include an internal marketing make-over. Frequently, IT is viewed as "the land of no." The modern IT leader needs to be able to enlighten and sell IT's offerings in marketing-speak. A tremendous amount of business value can be gained when IT becomes a strategic partner to marketing and the two work together on shared goals. The new tag line for IT should be "The Land of Know."

Strengthening the relationship between the CIO and the CMO is definitely an opportunity area for many companies; the question is, how deep will this extend? The IBM report poses several challenging questions:

- How closely are the CIOs and CMOs working together to personally realize common goals?

- How closely do the individual IT and marketing teams work together?

- Is there any cross training?

- Does anyone have the role of marketing technologist?

Forging a strong alliance is becoming increasingly important to reduce company costs and to tackle new opportunities such as driving business intelligence through analytics. How deeply will your company strengthen the relationship between IT and marketing?

From Captain to Coach, from Controlling to Enabling

I had an excellent conversation with Doug Harr recently. Doug is the CIO of Splunk, a leader in turning machine data into operational intelligence. Splunk is a fast-growing young company in a rapidly expanding part of the IT landscape. Machine data account for 90 percent of today's data, and it is critical for companies to develop capabilities for wresting meaningful insights from all of the data. For CIOs, that means adopting a new approach to innovation.

"Being an innovator in IT means opening your mind and being more of a partner than even before," says Doug. "In the past, we were in control and we made most of the decisions regarding IT. I tell people that today we've gone from being captain to being coach, from controlling to enabling. It might sound New Age, but it really makes a difference."

We have all heard about "big data," but relatively few executives feel comfortable about working with it. There are many unanswered questions, and a certain degree of confusion in the marketplace.

"I spend a lot of time explaining big data to business partners and clients," says Doug. "They want to understand the opportunity and the business value to their organizations. Big data analytics are very different from traditional BI [business intelligence], which most executives understand."

The emergence of business intelligence transformed the role of IT from purely operational into a blend of operational and strategic. BI essentially turned IT into a strategic weapon for the modern enterprise. Big data and predictive analytics are continuing that trend; they are elevating IT into a truly strategic role.

"Big data is creating new opportunities for innovation, in the same way that BI did in the previous decade," says Doug. "IT will play a prominent role as we move into this new transformational era of operational intelligence."

Big data analytics and operational intelligence offer a new way of looking at customer behavior—instead of guessing about it, you can see it happening in real time.

"Big data gives you the opportunity to really understand the customer experience at a much deeper level than we ever could in the past," says Doug. "It gives you a much clearer picture of how users, both internal and external, are experiencing your products and services. It brings together streams and feeds of data from many sources, and combines them into intelligence you can use to make better decisions, build better products, and improve the lives of your customers."

I really love how Doug envisions a world enabled and empowered by big data analytics. I also like his message that flexible IT leadership will be needed more than ever as we push further and deeper into the new world of big data.

Connecting the Dots Between Innovation and Analytics

I recently caught up with Brian Queenin, a partner at IBM who focuses on business analytics and optimization. Brian is a highly experienced consulting executive with truly global experience. Before he joined IBM, his posts included partner/enterprise performance management at Accenture, partner/vice president–global practice leader–business intelligence at Ernst & Young/Capgemini, and director of data warehousing at PricewaterhouseCoopers.

Brian is the real deal—a knowledgeable and deeply experienced thought leader. I am delighted that he has joined the team of expert sources contributing to this book.

I asked Brian to connect the dots between innovation, transformation, and analytics, and to speak briefly about the role of the CIO in ushering in a new era of big data and predictive analytics.

"Analytics will be the future heartbeat of the enterprise," he says. "We've traveled the road from decision support systems to data warehousing and business intelligence. The next step in this journey is analytics, and more specifically, predictive analytics."

Companies now rely on technology for "looking in the rearview mirror. We've been great at pulling together information from last week, last month, last quarter, and last year. We can look at the past with an extremely high level of accuracy."

What is important now, however, is developing the capabilities required to look ahead, to predict what will happen down the road. "Now we want to begin looking through the windshield. That rearview mirror is still useful, but it's not going to help us see the road in front of us."

Says Brian, "Predictive analytics takes the data that we already have in the enterprise and helps us digest it, understand it, siphon it off in manageable quantities, and use it to make better business decisions."

That is the potential of big data and predictive analytics—for the first time, we're using information to see more clearly what's ahead of us and adjust course based on what's likely to happen next in rapidly changing markets.

Brian continues: "If we stay in our silos with our blinders on, we won't see the future and we will be unprepared when it comes. [Management consultant] Peter Drucker once said,

'That which exists today is already old.' Most of the technologies we use today are yesterday's news. I read recently that 90 percent of the information that's available worldwide has been created in the past two years. What that means for a large organization is staggering. Today, information goes viral in minutes. Modern organizations need the ability to react much more quickly than ever before. Companies can no longer afford to wait months, weeks, or even hours before responding when something goes sideways. A brand, and even a company, can be severely damaged in a series of hours. The modern enterprise must have a finger on the pulse of their business outside their own four walls."

From Brian's perspective, the volume, velocity, variety, and veracity of big data are pushing the limits of Moore's Law.

"We're generating information at an alarming rate, but we're not developing the capabilities to digest that information," he says. "Information is being created faster than we can analyze it. As a result, the organization is becoming less intelligent. Our ability to digest and analyze information is diminishing compared to the rate at which new information is being created."

I also asked Brian what CIOs can do to up their game and prepare their team to handle this onslaught of data.

"I think they need to start with the burning questions," he says. "The biggest, hardest challenges are the best place to start, because they have an aura of excitement and importance around them. Going after low-hanging fruit doesn't necessarily get you the velocity-to-value that you need. Then bring in people who are experts in the field to assist with developing strategies, short-term approaches, and a long-term roadmap that can basically chart a path to success. Reach out with trust and confidence to advisors who can help you make a positive difference and transform the organization. You don't have to do it single-handedly."

The great promise of analytics, says Brian, is not spotting trends or boosting sales. The promise of analytics is using computers and software to change the future.

"Analytics gives us the capability to see what humans cannot easily see," he says. "Health-care analytics, for example, enables us to spot the onset of sepsis in infants 24 to 48 hours faster than ever before. That saves lives every day!"

I also asked Brian to offer some advice to CIOs who feel they have already fallen behind the curve.

"How do they get back in the game? They need to begin leading the revolution. At some point, the business will pull them into the revolution. If they are not already engaged, not already making the right moves, not already helping the business transform itself into what it needs to become, then someone else will take their place. That's a harsh message, but I think that's the reality."

I believe that Brian has neatly encapsulated the challenge: Today's CIO must be a leader. At this particular moment in history, leadership is critical and essential to long-term success.

Digging Deeper into Big Data

For a more comprehensive look at the phenomenon of big data, I turned to Michael Minelli, coauthor with Michele Chambers and Ambiga Dhiraj of *Big Data, Big Analytics*.[1]

Early in their book, the authors note that big data can be defined in several ways:

Big Data, as you might expect, is a relative term. Although many people define Big Data by volume, definitions of Big Data that are based on volume can be troublesome since some people define volume by the number of occurrences (in database terminology by the rows in a table or in analytics terminology known as the number of observations).

Some people define volume based on the number of interesting pieces of information for each occurrence (or in database terminology, the columns in a table, or in analytics terminology, the features or dimensions) and some people define volume by the combination of depth and width.

If you're a midmarket consumer packaged goods (CPG) company, you might consider 10 terabytes as Big Data. But if you're a multinational pharmaceutical corporation, then you would probably consider 500 terabytes as Big Data. If you're a three-letter government agency, anything less than a petabyte is considered small.

The industry has an evolving definition around Big Data that is currently defined by three dimensions: Volume, Variety and Velocity.

Clearly, big data is more than just lots of data. In addition to being "big," big data is also complex and fast. The image that comes to mind is a fire hose. The authors explain that even within the three dimensions of volume, variety, and velocity, there can be many variables:

> *Data volume can be measured by the sheer quantity of transactions, events, or amount of history that creates the data volume. . . . Typically, analytics have used smaller data sets called samples to create predictive models.*

Judging a data set from sample data can be like judging the size of an iceberg by looking at its tip!

> *By removing the data volume constraint and using larger data sets, enterprises can discover subtle patterns that can lead to targeted actionable microdecisions, or they can factor in more observations or variables into predictions that increases the accuracy of the predictive models.*
>
> *Data variety is the assortment of data. Traditionally data, especially operational data, is "structured" as it is put into a database based on the type of data (i.e., character, numeric, floating point, etc.). Over the past couple of decades, data has increasingly become "unstructured" as the sources of data have proliferated beyond operational applications.*
>
> *Text, audio, video, image, geospatial, Internet data (including click streams and log files) are considered unstructured data. However, since many of the sources of this data are programs, the data is in actuality*

"semi-structured." Semi-structured data is often a combination of different types of data. . . . For example, call center logs may contain customer name + date of call + complaint where the complaint information is unstructured and not easily synthesized into a data store.

Data velocity is about the speed at which data is created, accumulated, ingested, and processed. The increasing pace of world has put demands on businesses to process information in real-time or with near real-time responses. This may mean that data is processed on the fly or while "streaming" by to make quick, real-time decisions or it may be that monthly batch processes are run inter-day to produce more timely decisions.

The authors note that "unlike past eras in technology that were focused on driving down operational costs mostly through automation, the 'Analytics Age' has the potential to drive elusive top-line revenue for enterprises." Companies that learn how to leverage big data analytics will reap the rewards of lower operational costs and higher revenues, along with improved profit margins.

In summary, big data analytics combine a variety of analytic techniques to provide deeper insights, broader insights, and frictionless actions in which the insights are automatically converted into systematic actions generating tangible business results.

I recommend *Big Data, Big Analytics* as a valuable source of information on an emerging technology that will surely have a major impact on all of our lives.

Innovation in the Age of the Industrial Internet

Bill Ruh is vice president of global software and analytics at GE. I know, you are probably wondering when GE got into the software business. Technically, the company is doing the same thing it's been doing for the past 130 years: innovating, not for the sake of innovation, but for the benefits that innovation brings to the world. And as we all know, many of GE's innovations have also enjoyed spectacular commercial success.

A 30-year tech veteran and former Cisco executive, Bill now oversees GE's $1.5 billion software investment over the next three years and the company's new 125,000-square-foot "nerve center" in San Ramon, California. In his role, he is helping to mobilize more than 8,000 software engineers globally to speed the pace of innovation, collaboration, and commercialization of new technology to advance what some observers are already calling the "Age of the Industrial Internet." The industrial Internet is all about an open, global network that connects intelligent machines, people at work, and big data. It gives every machine not just a voice, but something powerful to say—the analytical intelligence to predict and prevent problems and get the right information to the right people at the right time. All of this requires continuous innovation.

Bill and his team are into so much cool stuff that it's hard to single out any one area for a quick discussion. That is why, for the purposes of this book, I am just going to focus on Bill's perspective on innovation itself. I asked Bill if he believes that true innovation results from a culture or a process. Here is a brief summary of his response:

> *Innovation occurs at many levels. You need a culture of intrapreneurship* [internal entrepreneurship] *to motivate and incentivize the creation and nurturing of new ideas and innovation, but you also need a process that will help the company manage those ideas. So innovation is initially about leadership, and then about management.*
>
> *The key is for leadership to create an environment where ideas can blossom—to excite our employees to become intrapreneurs. You need the management piece to make your innovation successful in the market. There's definitely a yin and yang—you really need both leadership and management.*

Bill's articulation of the innovation dilemma is spot on. It really got me thinking, and over the weekend I realized that you can look at innovation as a cycle with three distinct phases:

Phase I is top-down leadership support for a culture of innovation. If you don't have that, I don't see how you can call yourself an innovative company.

Phase II is bottom-up, grassroots innovation—people in the trenches and on the front lines generating great ideas.

Phase III is innovation management. This is the phase that most people would label as "the process," and it's absolutely crucial to keeping the cycle moving forward.

Phase III is where the ideas meet reality. Some ideas will be judged more worthy than others. A handful of ideas will survive, many will die.

In its totality, the three-part cycle becomes your culture of innovation. It combines top-down leadership, grassroots passion, and the business savvy of experienced managers.

In a very real sense, Bill and his team at GE are creating more than new products for the world—they are creating a new worldview. You do not need to be a venture-backed start-up in order to innovate.

Moving Toward the Customer

Most CIOs agree that operational excellence and innovation are two prime areas in which success is imperative.

But there is a third area in which some CIOs are expected to excel: customer management. This third area—or third mandate, if you will—is becoming increasingly important as products and services become increasingly dependent on technology. If what you are selling is technology, it makes perfect sense for the CIO to be involved in the customer management process.

To be fair, I think we are mostly talking about business-to-business (B2B) scenarios here, in which the CIO is brought into a meeting with a customer or prospective customer for the purpose of helping the sales executives accelerate the sales process or close a deal.

But CIOs can also help sales and marketing teams explain the value of sophisticated technologies. After all, a prospective customer is likely to view the CIO as a credible expert in technology—especially when the CIO's company is actually using the products or services being sold.

As mentioned earlier, CIOs should understand their company's customers and competitors as well as (or preferably *better than*) CMOs and vice presidents of sales. Additionally, CIOs should focus more on bringing innovation to market. It's important to remember that markets are made up of customers. CIOs should do their utmost to understand the needs and preferences of customers, since customers are the generators of revenue and profit. There is no question that the idea of a customer-facing CIO makes more sense in some situations than in others. If the product you offer is primarily intended for consumers—take the Apple iPhone, for example—then you do not need to include the CIO in the sales process.

But when the product or service is highly complex and technology-dependent—let's say it's a pharmacy benefits management service or a data security management service—then it makes good business sense to bring the CIO into the sales process.

Not every CIO will feel comfortable taking on a sales role. But some CIOs tell me that they enjoy their customer-facing responsibilities because interacting with customers gives them a much better understanding of the world that exists outside of the IT organization.

That improved level of understanding helps the CIO do a better job of serving the company's customers, which in turn helps the company. All told, it's a great example of a virtuous cycle in which the CIO can—and should—play a critical role.

I firmly believe that transformational CIOs have a responsibility to serve as leaders, both inside and outside of IT. Helping sales and marketing boost the company's top-line performance is a perfect way for the CIO to demonstrate his or her C-level leadership capabilities.

Lining Up the Innovation Roadmaps

Chris McGugan is vice president and general manager of emerging products and technologies at Avaya. He leads teams of brilliant minds whose focus is on creating new and useful products and services. Prior to joining Avaya, he worked at Belkin and Cisco, two companies with rich histories of innovation.

In a very literal sense, Chris is a true master of innovation. In his role at Avaya, he is a generational link in a long and respected chain of innovation that traces its roots directly back to Bell Laboratories and the legendary Alexander Graham Bell.

Chris leads a group with an amazing degree of cross-functional expertise and experience. Specialties range from database architecture scalability to enterprise collaboration communication systems, from pure research to programming.

"One of the guys on our team wrote a book that was assigned reading when I was in college," says Chris.

When I caught up with Chris, I asked him how his group maintains and supports its culture of continuous discovery and innovation.

"It's something you have to drive toward," he says. "It's not enough to just say, 'We're an innovation company, voilà!' and it's more than a question of having the right cultural DNA."

I think that what Chris is saying is that while it certainly helps to have more than 65 PhD-level people on staff, the hard part is prioritizing their efforts and making the right decisions about which projects to nurture and which projects to kill.

"There's a funnel process you have to go through to figure out what you're going to invest in and what you're not going to invest in," says Chris. "Some decisions are based on data and some decisions are based on gut feelings. The process can make you a little crazy, but it's a constant cycle."

Chris explains that his group serves as "an in-house VC [venture capital] firm, where we'll do as much statistical and data analysis on a particular idea and make sure it fits within the confines of reasonableness. Then we work it through with real customers."

I love the idea of an "in-house VC firm"—it's simply brilliant, and it makes perfect sense from a business perspective.

"It's almost like our version of Kickstarter [a company that provides innovative tools for raising capital]," says Chris. "We bring together technologists from some of our largest clients and some of our smallest clients, we spend one or two days talking through what we're thinking about investing in and showing them demonstrations of new products."

After a customer, or a group of customers, has expressed a real interest in the new product or service, Chris and his team will make the decision to move forward with an additional investment.

The critical part of this process is keeping the focus on products and services that customers really want. The primary focus is on external factors such as market conditions and customer demand.

For Chris, it's absolutely essential to keep his teams aware of the real world outside the laboratory. To make sure that an "inside/outside" balance is maintained, innovation teams meet routinely with clients and customers to exchange information, share experiences, and see how new products work in the field.

That's a useful detail and a great takeaway. You don't want your innovation teams to work in a vacuum. You need to make it possible and convenient for them to meet with customers and users. Having that kind of process in place and making it routine will substantially reduce the chances of an unwanted surprise when a new product or service is unveiled.

Synchronizing the development of new technologies is another part of innovation leadership. An "easy" question facing innovation leaders might look something like this:

If you've got a development budget of $6,000 and you're developing 12 new products, and each new product has a relative value of $1,000, where do spend your money?

A more complex version of that question looks like this:

If you've got a development budget of $6,000 and you're developing 12 new products, and each new product has a relative value of $1,000, and you have 4 clients willing to buy new products in the next 6 months and 6 clients willing to buy new products in the next 12 months, where do spend your money?

"It's quite intriguing to see how the client requirement roadmap lines up with our development roadmap. But lining up those roadmaps is helpful for gauging our investment time horizon," Chris explains. "If we've decided we're going to invest in 12 new products, then maybe we will accelerate four projects and decelerate the others to make the roadmaps line up. This has been a very effective means for us to hone the innovation curve and meet the expectations of our customers."

Again, I admire the way Chris keeps the focus of his group's efforts on the real world outside the lab. That's a hallmark, I believe, of true innovation leaders.

Designing Practical Innovation Strategies

I had a very enlightening conversation with Dr. Françoise LeGoues in which she reminded me that innovation comes in many shapes and sizes. Françoise is vice president of CIOLab, Office of the CIO at IBM. In her role, she spends a lot of time thinking about innovation and devising practical strategies for achieving it.

She pointed out that when we think of innovation, we tend to think of supremely transformative innovations such as the light bulb, penicillin, or digital photography. But not every innovation has to be monumental in scale.

"Many people think of innovation as a new gadget or a new technology. But that's not what constitutes innovation," says Françoise. "At IBM we say that innovation is the intersection of invention and insight. Innovation happens when you find a new way to solve a problem."

Sometimes you're solving a big problem that's been around for a long time. In the field of medicine, for example, diabetes had been a huge problem for thousands of years. The discovery of insulin was a huge leap forward for mankind, a truly major innovation that changed the world.

Not every innovation has to be earth-shattering, however. Sometimes a small innovation can open a door or inspire people's imagination, which then leads to a series of innovations. In many instances, innovations are modest improvements to existing products or systems.

"For example, what does this year's smartphone do that last year's smartphone cannot do? The difference between the two isn't huge, but it represents a process of continuous improvement through innovation," says Françoise. "When you apply innovation to supply chain optimization, you might get a 1 percent or 2 percent improvement in efficiency. But those incremental improvements can add up quickly, and in today's economy, supply chain efficiency is a competitive advantage."

I asked Françoise how CIOs can become transformation leaders of innovation in their organizations. From her perspective, the hardest part of transformational leadership isn't technology. "Changing the organization's culture is often harder than changing its technology," she says. "In the past, the senior executives would go out, study the market, and come back with ideas for how to change things. It was a top-down process, with a strict hierarchy. That's not the way innovation happens today. In today's interconnected and networked economy, the best ideas often bubble up from the bottom, sometimes from the youngest or most junior people in the organization."

Given the new realities of the global economy, it makes sense for organizations to have structures and processes for capturing ideas at the grassroots level.

"You need a structure that listens to the wisdom of the crowd," says Françoise. "You need to be flexible, so you can react quickly to what is happening around you at an incredible rate of speed. You really need to listen to the world, listen to the people in your organization, and embrace the change."

Until fairly recently, it was possible to "make the right decision by either studying the problem or being very smart," says Françoise. Today's world is far too complex and moves too quickly for that kind of approach.

"You need a really strong structure of innovation and strong programs that can look at what's happening, and then—quickly, flexibly, and cheaply—test a lot of things and see which takes off. The size of your organization doesn't matter. What matters is whether you have a structure for spotting innovation and reacting quickly so you don't miss opportunities. That's what really counts."

Generally, an innovation life cycle has five stages:

1. Identify the challenge

2. Brainstorm and share ideas

3. Incubate and collaborate

4. Validate and iterate

5. Implement and go to market

Within each stage, the innovation process moves from "inside" to "outside," meaning that as ideas transform from vision to reality, they move closer to users and markets. The progression from "inside" to "outside" at each stage helps keep innovation projects on track and on target to deliver real value.

It is a complex process, but "it makes the point that there is no such thing as 'one big innovation program' that can support the big and small innovations and the transformative strategy," says Françoise. "You're not talking about one program. Instead, you are talking about mapping different programs to cover the entire space. That way, you can support several innovations with multiple and overlaid programs. Together they create what I would call a true innovation strategy."

Managing Between Extremes

Despite its complexity, the process avoids two common extremes of innovation management that are referred to by research and advisory firm Gartner as "death by management selection" and "death by natural selection." Either extreme can be a trap, Françoise explains.

"'Death by management selection' means that somebody has a good idea, goes to a manager, the manager says 'yay' or 'nay.' It's a perfectly good way to manage innovation in a start-up company where you have a small team and the CEO is the one closest to the needs of the company," says Françoise.

"'Death by natural selection' means that you let the people test your ideas. The winners are selected by the wisdom of the crowd, and by people's behavior, not by a manager. The Internet lets you do that. But how do you put a system in place that lets everyone evaluate all the ideas? In a complex enterprise, that can be difficult."

Based on my experience, the best choice would to plot a course between the two extremes. You want to include as many voices and opinions as possible in the innovation process. But you can't abdicate your responsibilities as a manager, which means that at some point in the process you will have to decide which projects move forward and which projects are canceled.

Three Complementary Pairs of Roles

Citing the IBM 2011 CIO Study, Françoise also mentioned the need for bringing new sets of skills and capabilities to the table. Be prepared to play multiple roles and wear several hats. CIOs who are successful leaders of innovation combine three distinct pairs of roles, she says.

"They are insightful visionaries and able pragmatists, savvy value creators and relentless cost cutters, and collaborative business leaders and inspiring IT managers. Those pairs might seem contradictory, but they are actually complementary. By integrating those three pairs of roles, the CIO makes innovation real, raises the ROI of IT, and expands business impact."

Note

1. Michael Minelli, Michele Chambers, and Ambiga Dhiraj, *Big Data, Big Analytics: Emerging Business Intelligence and Analytic Trends for Today's Businesses* (Hoboken, NJ: John Wiley & Sons, 2013).

Chapter 7

Why Credible Leadership Matters

Since innovation is a key driver of success in modern markets, all senior-level executives should consider themselves partners in the company's innovation efforts. As members of the C-suite, CIOs play crucial roles as both enablers and leaders of innovation.

It is important to remember that innovation begins and ends with people. If you want to become a leader of innovation, first you must become a leader of people.

People follow leaders they trust. That means you need to work on building trust with the people in your organization, and especially with your colleagues in the C-suite. CIOs who cannot build trusting relationships with their CEOs and CFOs simply will not have the resources or credibility required to support innovation strategies.

We have heard the term "people, process, and technology" so often that we tend to forget how relevant it is in today's business environments. Build those bridges to people first. If you do not get the people part right, the process and technology won't matter.

It is all about leadership—when you have trusting relationships with people, they will follow you to the ends of the earth. We relearn this simple lesson with every new era of technology development. People enable your success. Technology is important, but you cannot succeed without the loyalty and support of people who trust you.

Success in today's markets requires speed, agility, and flexibility. You need teams of people who can turn on a dime, shift gears, and move rapidly in new directions.

The convergence of multiple trends—cloud, social, mobile, big data, and security—is driving an epic revolution. We have the tools, the platforms, and the networks required to innovate at unparalleled speed. We can turn business vision into business reality faster than ever before.

This is truly the most exciting time to be in the information technology industry. Far from being mature, the IT industry is still young. People are counting on us to provide leadership. We cannot let them down.

Friends, we are in the first inning of a nine-inning game. We have only just begun!

Do Not Hesitate to Be a Leader

Frank Slootman is president and CEO of ServiceNow, a leading provider of cloud-based services that automate enterprise IT operations. Prior to joining ServiceNow, Frank served as a venture partner with Greylock Partners, a venture capital firm. From July 2003 to July 2009, Frank served as president and CEO of Data Domain, an electronic storage solution company that was acquired by EMC Corporation in 2009.

Clearly, Frank knows the technology playing field and understands the challenges facing CIOs and their companies. In a recent conversation, he offered some excellent advice for CIOs and senior IT leaders.

"Many CIOs are in a defensive mode. They feel like they're under siege mode and fighting to stay alive from day to day," observes Frank. As a result, they tend to focus on protecting the status quo. But that's a mistake, he says.

"It's far better to be proactive. Have a roadmap showing exactly where you plan to go. When you are the CIO, you cannot adopt a wait-and-see attitude. You have to go in with a very clear and specific agenda of transformational change," says Frank. "You need to be moving away from the status quo, not presiding over it."

The life of a CIO can be difficult, because IT operations often appear mysterious to outsiders. Even when senior executives don't understand precisely how IT works, they understand that money is being spent, and they hold the CIO accountable when they don't believe that IT is generating value.

Avoiding that scenario requires advance planning and preparation. "The CIO has to be in the driver's seat, setting the agenda and establishing realistic goals. Don't let other people set the baselines. The CIO should be the one who declares victory," counsels Frank.

Frank sees cloud-based services as a logical part of the CIO's strategy. Leveraging the cloud's ability to provide "pay by the drink" infrastructure services can make it easier for CIOs to spend more time focusing on value creation, and less time worrying about keeping the lights on.

"I believe that cloud is a necessary evolution," says Frank. "The amount of compute that has to be delivered to the world over the next 10 to 20 years is tremendous, and there aren't enough system administrators and database administrators and network security people to manage that kind of infrastructure model. So we have to go to a completely different model. For most CIOs, that means they're not going to be running infrastructure. It means they're going to be buying compute the same way they're buying power, dial tone, and bandwidth—by the drink."

Frank raises a great point. But if the infrastructure goes away, what becomes of the CIO? "If the infrastructure is behind the curtain then your focus is going to be internal delivery, workflow automation, and really understanding how technology can change and affect the business in a way that the business actually notices," says Frank. "Instead of spending most of your time tending infrastructure, you're going to spend 90 percent of your time understanding how technology affects the business. That means your focus is at application level, not at the infrastructure level."

I genuinely appreciate the way in which Frank frames the issues, challenges, and opportunities. Clearly, the CIO should be setting the transformation agenda and calling the shots. Sometimes the best defense is a great offense.

Sometimes Getting Out of the Way Is the First Step to Achieving Innovation

I recently had the pleasure of speaking with Tim Dilley, the executive vice president of services at NetSuite. Tim oversees NetSuite's global initiatives in professional services, training, and customer support. Prior to joining NetSuite, he served as senior vice president of global customer services at Informatica Corp.

Tim's experience and expertise as an executive leader in professional services and customer support makes him a great resource for discussing how the cloud impacts innovation in the modern enterprise.

I asked Tim to describe how successful IT leaders leverage the cloud to spur innovation and drive transformational strategies at their companies.

"Cloud computing is really about enabling companies to invest in expansion," he says. "Let's say your company is launching a new business in Asia. As the CIO, you're responsible for delivering IT services to the new business. You don't have the time to do it the old-fashioned way. You can't spend three years building out infrastructure. You need it fast. So instead of buying infrastructure, you buy the applications you need in a cloud-based services model. Then you can go back to the board and say, 'IT is ready.' Essentially, you've gotten out of the way. You've removed the potential friction."

I really like the way Tim describes the basic concept of leveraging the cloud to remove the classic obstacles that can slow expansion into new markets. Buying apps in the cloud enables you to leap over the infrastructure hurdle and concentrate on delivering critical services where and when they're really needed.

"Now the company can make investments and not worry about how long it will take to build the IT infrastructure," he says. "From my perspective, the cloud enables business growth by removing many of the old problems."

I think this is the right way to look at the cloud. Instead of seeing the cloud as a new kind of technology, it's important to see its potential as a critical enabler of business strategy.

In today's rapidly changing markets, speed is absolutely essential. You need to get up and running fast—before your competition beats you to the draw. At the same time, you're facing higher levels of risk. The cloud allows you to move rapidly and spend minimally. From my point of view, that's a great combination!

Acting quickly and minimizing risk are prerequisites for competing successfully in modern markets. I believe that Tim is spot on in his assessment of how the cloud can play a significant role in business innovation and strategic growth.

"A key part of innovation is simply getting out of the way and enabling people to do what they need to do," he says. "If you can remove the obstacles, you are making a difference."

Innovation Conundrum

Dave Smoley was recently appointed CIO at AstraZeneca, a global biopharmaceutical company. When we interviewed him for this book, he was the SVP and CIO at Flextronics, a global supplier to the electronics manufacturing and design industry. Despite its status as a Fortune 500 company, Flextronics tends to act more like a smaller business when it comes to innovation. The company is agile and entrepreneurial. In today's fast-paced economy, those qualities are essential.

In his role as a technology leader, Dave is perfectly positioned to see both sides of what he calls the "innovation conundrum." Here's an edited summary of what he said in our interview:

Too much standardization can stifle innovation. Too little standardization can drive up costs. So you need to find a balance.

You also need clear business drivers. You don't want to innovate just for the sake of innovating. You need to align innovation with your organizational mission and goals.

Keep your strategic innovation focused on customer demands and business requirements. Use innovation to find cheaper, faster ways of solving problems.

Great companies create a culture that inspires creativity and innovation across the enterprise, says Dave:

If you create a mentality and a culture around innovation, then you can innovate all over the place. Innovation can happen throughout the organization.

You want to create a culture where people think innovatively all the time, where innovation is like breathing. The traditional way of thinking about innovation was that it had to be a special activity. People said, "I can't innovate because I don't have time to innovate," or "I can't innovate because I don't have a budget for innovation."

That kind of thinking is nonsense. In fact, it's been proven that restricting resources actually drives innovation. If you follow many of the great innovations at Apple, you'll find that many of them resulted from restrictions and constraints. Steve Jobs would tell the engineers about a new product he had imagined and they would tell him it was impossible and then he would tell them that he wanted to see a prototype on Monday. And they would spend the weekend devising some amazing new product!

Dave offers great advice for creating and sustaining a culture of innovation:

Encourage small experiments and nurture curiosity. Make it okay to fail. Kill bad ideas early, and then move on. Reward good ideas and encourage their adoption.

Accelerating Innovation Through Partnerships

In the preceding section, we heard from Dave Smoley in his role as CIO. Now we will hear from Dave in his role as the cocreator of The Innovative CIO, an executive education course taught at the Stanford University Graduate School of Business. Dave launched this program with his CIO peer and friend Brian Lillie, CIO at Equinix. The Innovative CIO program teaches concepts for creating and sustaining an innovative culture in an enterprise IT organization.

I recently asked Dave to share his insights about the value of partnering to accelerate innovation that leads to competitive advantages for the business.

"It's extremely important for the CIO to take an active leadership role in the development of partnerships that will help the organization innovate," he says. "It takes commitment, time, and energy to find and engage the right partners. But the experience of partnering can be highly invigorating, stimulating, and exciting. Partnering is essential, and the CIO should play a prominent role in building a network of trusted partners for the organization."

Dave recommends that CIOs lead the partnering process and remain personally involved. "There's a lot of networking involved. Partnering is all about collaboration, openness, sharing, interdependence, and integrity. Those are the leadership qualities that come to mind when we talk about partnering."

CIO's wanting to create and sustain a culture of innovative thinking will be more successful if they look for ways to partner with smaller, more nimble companies. "Many of the smaller companies that create new technologies are led by supersmart people who are on the leading edge and pushing the edge out further," says Dave. "At the Stanford program we train executives to continuously scan the landscape and look for partners who can help them solve problems. There are companies out there with the expertise and the technology you need, but you have to be looking for them."

Dave suggests creating a process and a culture that encourages and rewards identifying potential partners. "You have to personally invest time and develop relationships. You need to figure out which companies are worth spending time with. You need to create an ongoing dialogue within your organization that helps you narrow down the list of potential partners and eventually guides you toward the right partner—or team of partners—to solve the problem."

Through that process and methodology, you can selectively decide to spend time with a handful of companies. "Many of the companies you're looking at are probably small, early-stage companies and they don't have a lot of resources," says Dave. "You have to be respectful of that. You need to be ready to tell them, 'This isn't going to work, it's not a fit for us,' or 'Thank you, let's talk in a year and see where you are,' or 'Let's figure out how we can do a pilot or some sort of experiment.'"

Dave says that he encourages his team to send him e-mails "at any hour of the day or night" when they find a company that might be a good fit. "I spend a lot of my time scanning the landscape and developing relationships," he says. "Sometimes I come back from a meeting with two or three pages of notes that I pass along to my team. I believe that it's important to share what you learn and keep everyone in the loop. I'll ask my team, 'What do you know about this company? What have you heard?'"

The advantage of Dave's approach is that it builds a "rhythm" and sets clear level of expectation. "My team understands if I'm suggesting something, there's a good reason. I'm not saying, 'Drop everything you're doing and go after this.' But in general, I expect the team to respond within a relatively short period of time and I expect them to think out of the box. They need to be open-minded but also candid and honest. I've found that building a rhythm actually speeds up the process. Sometimes the response is, 'Yeah, we've met with those guys and we don't like them,' and sometimes the response is, 'We've had a meeting, we like them, and they might be a good partner.' That's how we like to operate. We have agility and we're open-minded. Those qualities enable us to move fast, avoid distractions, and make decisions quickly."

Moving quickly also reduces the chances that new ideas will be killed because they don't fit neatly into the existing infrastructure.

"It's back to the innovation conundrum that we talked about before, which is about finding a balance between standardization and flexibility. Traditionally, IT shops have been built around standardization, rules, and compliance. You had to dictate which devices and which software we would—and would not—use in the enterprise," explains Dave. "What's happening now is that consumerization has beaten down those walls, and we've had to become more flexible. We've transformed ourselves from the guys who say no into the guys who say yes. The upside is that we can act much more quickly and effectively, especially when we're scanning the world around us to find partners."

Dave likens partners to stocks in a portfolio. "You have somewhere between 4 to 10 core partners that you're dealing with on a regular basis. Then you have 20 to 30 smaller partners that you are moving in and out of the portfolio, based on your needs."

Partnering with smaller companies also helps avoid the temptation to rely on "skunk works" to deal with unmet technology needs. From Dave's perspective, modern innovation is not about "the guy who finds some cool technology, creates a little pet project, and then goes off by himself to develop it."

Modern innovation, says Dave, is driven by "a conversation occurring up and down the organization, a conversation about what's interesting, what's exciting, and what's working. It is a conversation that extends horizontally across the organization and between departments."

I would add that it is also a conversation involving partners and potential partners outside of the organization. I think the moral of this story is that you have got to be willing to go beyond traditional boundaries—internally and externally— to solve problems. When agility and speed are required for success, the traditional method of testing, buying, and implementing enterprise-level solutions is too expensive and takes too much time. That does not eliminate the need for traditional vendors; it just means that in some situations, going with a nontraditional vendor might be the right choice.

"In the past, partnering with a start-up was considered too risky for a large company," says Dave. "But the cloud enables lots of start-ups to deliver products and services at much lower costs and with less risk. Today, you can start a legitimate company, build legitimate products, and begin delivering value without huge investments of time and money. That represents a big difference from the past. Today, you can partner with smaller companies that will help you deploy complex enterprise systems globally, in multiple languages, in less than a year. That's the value of finding good partners, whether they're small or large."

A Shifting Mindset

In many respects, the use of cloud as a development and infrastructure platform has changed the rules of the game. Dave explains,

We've got so many cloud tools in our core enterprise architecture that we're shifting our whole mindset around how we work with these vendors. They come out with three upgrades per year, whether you want it or not. They're

constantly moving to new stuff. It's a much more dynamic environment, which means the business and the IT organization have got to shift from the old mindset that said, "Let's lock this down, optimize it, and at some point five or six years from now, when it makes financial sense, we will launch a project and do a major refresh." That old mindset is giving way to a new mindset that takes into account that companies are innovating rapidly and constantly changing their products. You can no longer control the pace of change. Instead, you need a roadmap so you can understand where the technology is going, and you need a process for keeping up. Operating in this brave new world of continual change can be challenging. Sometimes you take two steps forward and one step backward.

Innovative vendors such as Salesforce.com, Workday, and ServiceNow "add major chunks of capability and functionality three times a year," says Dave. "You have to understand their roadmap and figure out how to best respond. It might involve training, it might involve change management. For sure it will involve testing. In any event, you will need a process for adapting to change, integrating change, and moving forward smoothly. That's the challenge—and the opportunity—of continuous innovation. The days of three-year IT strategies are over. Today, you have to be comfortable with change and you have to be comfortable leading your organization through a changing world."

Dave notes correctly that in the past, dealing with change was often delegated or outsourced. That is simply no longer the case.

"Senior IT leadership must be involved in the innovation space. It's critical. In the past, when you heard about a new technology or new vendor, [you would] mention it to someone in your organization and say, 'Take a look at this and get back to me if it's interesting.' Then you would forget about it. You would assume that if it was something worth pursuing, somehow it would resurface. You cannot operate like that today. You have to be proactive and you have to provide leadership."

Toward the end of our conversation, I asked Dave to provide a quick top-line summary of his thoughts on the new CIO mindset. Here is his summary:

Make it a priority to create a culture of innovation. You have to decide it's important to your team and to your success, and you must consciously dedicate time and energy to it.

Your innovation process must have clear business drivers. You must align your efforts with the mission of the company and the organization.

Pick the pieces of your existing infrastructure that you can replace or unwind as you begin moving to a new and more flexible infrastructure. Pick areas in which you can experiment, where you can fail fast.

Learn how to partner with growth-stage companies. Try something different. Don't be afraid to break the old model.

I truly believe that Dave has formulated a winning approach and great philosophy of leadership. I am especially impressed that in a true spirit of collaboration, he has shared his thoughts so generously with us.

Leading Innovation and Driving Transformation

Today's CIO is uniquely positioned to lead innovation and drive transformation across the modern enterprise. That is an indisputable fact.

The real question is this: Will CIOs seize the day? Will they leverage their opportunities to become truly transformational leaders?

Naturally, I am hoping that CIOs will step up and demonstrate their leadership abilities. My hope is based on more than my own personal interest in seeing CIOs succeed. It is based on my firm belief that successful companies need transformational CIOs. It is really that simple. I cannot think of a successful company today that does not have a great IT team and great IT leadership.

In today's economy, business and IT are inseparable. You cannot have one without the other.

Innovation is the driving force of business growth. It is also the engine of transformation. CIOs can—and should—take responsibility for driving transformational strategies leading to business success.

The three of the most important strategic resources required for continuous change and improvement already reside within the IT portfolio: mobile, social, and cloud computing.

This is a singular moment in the history of information technology. The CIO is responsible for three incredibly powerful levers of transformation. That is not an exaggeration. It is the truth.

Mobile, social, and cloud computing are game changers. Taken together, they are fundamentally rearranging human culture. CIOs can play a key role in this amazing global transformation. Or they can sit on the sideline and let others run with the ball.

Now is the time for CIOs to seize the day. Be the rock stars, be the heroes, be the transformational leaders.

You can do it. If you are an IT executive, you are uniquely qualified to provide leadership in the modern enterprise. Step up and enjoy your moment in the sun. You deserve it.

Managing the Merger of Culture and Technology

Arthur McAdams is director of graduate studies at the School of Business, University of Bridgeport. Earlier in his career, Art was senior vice president and director of information systems at People's Bank (now People's United), one of the nation's stronger regional banks and a recognized leader in innovation.

As an educator and former IT executive, Art clearly sees innovation as a merger of culture and technology, with the emphasis on culture. "Culture is the most important enabler and driver of innovation," he says. "A culture of innovation should be defined, embraced, and promoted by the CEO. A culture of innovation includes a long-term and continuous commitment of educating and supporting all stakeholders."

Art makes a strong case for a long-term strategy of innovation. A culture of innovation is more than a single project or program; it has to be lasting and continuous. It should also be something that is perceived as inherently valuable, and not seen as a passing fad or momentary trend.

"The long-term health and success of an organization requires continuous adjustments in competitive positioning, which in turn require both incremental and radical improvements," he says. "Successful organizations find a balance between stability and agility. Too much disruption will lead to chaos, but too much emphasis on stability will lead to stagnation."

Every employee has unique gifts, says Art, and those gifts should be recognized and used properly. That being said, not all employees feel the same way about continuous change and adaptation. "Some employees prefer stability, while others prefer the challenges of being agile. Both kinds of employees are necessary."

The key management task is creating an environment where appropriate risk is accepted and even encouraged. In that kind of environment, there is a perceived difference between a "mistake" and a production error. Mistakes are expected and tolerated; errors are not. Art reminded me of Peter Drucker's famous line: "People who don't take risks generally make about two big mistakes a year. People who do take risks generally make about two big mistakes a year."

Thornton May, Clayton Christensen, and other innovation thought leaders have noted that traditional return on investment (ROI) metrics can stifle projects that fall outside of the usual parameters for measuring incremental linear improvements. Constant tactical and task-oriented reviews of ROI during a long-term strategic innovation effort will often hinder the desired outcome. That danger can arise, says Art, when chief financial officers hold disproportionate influence in organizations.

"CIOs need to make the business case to the CEO that lack of innovation can lead to corporate demise in the form of irrelevance and perpetual cost pressure," says Art. "A certain fiscally responsible amount of money should be allocated for new development that skirts the usual ROI methods for acceptance."

From Art's perspective, the management challenge is capturing initial flashes of brilliance and moving them through a usual formal series of steps to realize the goal of creating a new product, service, or process. "There are plenty of great daydreamers who have nothing to show for their work," says Art. "The key is having a culture that supports continuous innovation and understands its value to the organization."

Two Tiers of IT Innovation in the Modern Global Enterprise

I had a great conversation recently with Jonathan Landon. Jonathan is responsible for global IT strategy, technology, and architecture at Kimberly-Clark, and his insights on innovation are especially valuable.

From Jonathan's perspective, ability scale plays an important role in determining the eventual success or failure of an innovation. An innovative solution that costs $4 million and delivers great value for your largest business or at corporate level might not deliver value at the local or regional level, where a $40,000 investment might be much more appropriate.

"Certain business processes are very dissimilar around the world," says Jonathan. "You cannot assume, for example, that a customer-facing process that works well in North America will work as effectively in an emerging market. That kind of assumption might result in a costly mistake."

Instead of reaching reflexively for the global solution, think first of whether it will fit across the many parts of your enterprise. "In some cases, you're just going to have to accept a two-tier solution," says Jonathan. "You may have to have a tier that is appropriate for your large business units and another tier that is appropriate for your smaller business units. The key idea here is to start small and scale it up, rather than starting big and then trying to make it smaller—scaling down rarely works."

Jonathan and his team at Kimberly-Clark have developed a process they call "Business Capability Road Mapping" to predict the technology needs of the company's many business units all over the world as they continue growing into new or expanding markets. They use the insights gained from the roadmapping process to help their vendors focus on developing products and services that will support the company's strategic vision as a global organization. They use the same process to plan the next generation of skills that the IT organization needs to drive rapid value realization.

Getting the vendors on board early helps avoid last-minute scrambles that can result in unwieldy or overcomplex solutions. "Our perspective is that if it's not easy to use, then it probably won't generate the value required by the business case," says Jonathan. "Even if it has all the features and functionality, it has to be easy to use. Usability trumps functionality."

This is a refreshing departure from the conventional wisdom of the past two decades, in which user needs were not generally given priority and CIOs assumed that enterprise-wide IT systems were inherently more effective than regional or country-wide systems. While those assumptions might have proven correct in Europe and North America, they are being challenged in new markets emerging in the BRIC nations (Brazil, Russia, India, and China).

For Jonathan, the role of IT in driving business value brings new excitement to the profession. "I've been here at Kimberly-Clark for 31 years. But when I come to work these days, I feel like a kid," he says. "Almost everything I've been working for all these years has come to fruition. Today, IT innovation is central to business success in the marketplace. It's an absolutely wonderful time to be an IT leader."

A Role Model for Innovation and Leadership

Recently I had the good fortune of chatting with Brian R. Lurie, the VP and CIO of Teleflex Incorporated, a leading global provider of specialty medical devices for a range of procedures in critical care and surgery.

I have known Brian for quite a while, and I was delighted to speak with him again. Brian is one of those rare corporate leaders who can blend traditional values with a real instinct for driving business results.

Prior to joining Teleflex, Brian served for more than a decade as vice president of IT at Stryker Orthopaedics, the largest operating division of Stryker Corp. and a global leader in the design, development, manufacturing, marketing, and sales of reconstructive, trauma, and sports medicine orthopedic products and services.

In addition to his IT role, Brian was a founding member of Stryker's Business Technology Council, a cross-divisional corporate group whose primary responsibility was making sure that Stryker was leveraging technology to grow the business and achieve the company's strategic goals.

Brian's experience serving on senior-level executive teams gives him a truly unique insight into the business challenges facing modern corporations in high-velocity markets. When we spoke, I asked him about the CIO's role as an innovation leader. Here is a brief summary of what he told me:

As a driver of innovation, the CIO should be a leader and a role model. The CIO should talk about the types of innovation that are important to the organization. The CIO should also model the behaviors that support a culture of innovation. In other words, the CIO should walk the talk.

But in addition to being a role model, the CIO needs to honor the spirit of innovation and make sure that innovation is rewarded. That's an important piece of the process—you need to reward people for being innovative if you want them to innovate. That's human nature.

You also need to remember that your people are watching you all the time. They watch you closely. They know when you're serious about something and they know when you're just going through the motions. If you're not serious about supporting innovation, they'll know it and their actions will reflect your true feelings.

However, if you show them that you genuinely appreciate innovation and that you are willing to make sure that innovation is rewarded, they will follow your example. That is how a culture of innovation works, from my perspective.

Brian's wisdom reflects and reinforces my own belief that successful IT organizations are built around innovation. Today, much of that innovation is focused on leveraging mobile, social, and cloud technologies to drive business growth. But the technologies themselves are less important than the innovations they enable.

Technologies come and go—great CIOs focus on creating value for the business through leadership, innovation, and transformation. From my vantage point, that's the role of the modern CIO.

The Next Big Wave: IT Value Creation

In Chapter 4's "Eight Action Steps for Driving Innovation," my friend Tom Fountain provided us with a detailed list of actionable innovation steps. I spoke with Tom again recently and asked him to outline his vision for the next big wave in IT. Here is a brief summary of what he told me:

We're in a new era of IT evolution, the era of IT value creation. This is the era in which IT is judged by its impact on the business. The previous era was largely dominated by investments in enterprise resource planning (ERP) transformation projects.

Many of those ERP projects delivered on their promises, but there was also a lot of disappointment, mostly because people could not get the business intelligence they needed. Sure, the new systems could tell you how many orders you had and show you your inventory, but they didn't deliver the kind of insight you need to make great business decisions.

Today, everyone is talking about big data analytics. They are also useful, but my guess is that people will find analytics disappointing for many of the same reasons they found ERP systems disappointing.

Here's my point: People want systems that tell them "how" and not just "what." In today's hypercompetitive markets, knowing more about your customers isn't enough—you also have to know how to act on that knowledge. The analytics can tell you "what" your customers want, but they can't tell you how to develop, price, market, produce, and deliver it.

That is why the next big wave is something beyond just analytics. The next big wave will be the orchestration of business across a value chain that is both virtual and highly distributed.

The next big challenge for CIOs—and for all parts of the business—is making sure that all the processes are orchestrated and optimized, across all the various parts of the enterprise and its network of partners. That is how IT will create value, through the dynamic orchestration of technologies and processes.

More specifically, IT will help the business sense, interpret, and successfully respond to "events" going on around it—even during execution—in ways that preserve the original intent of the business and sustain, or even improve, the business outcome.

IT's ability to organize and orchestrate business process execution—and to provide feedback that can be used to improve results—will become an increasingly critical function within the modern enterprise.

Wow, I think Tom hit the nail on the head. I really like how he defines the new era of IT value creation. Big data analytics are part of the solution, no doubt, but what the business really wants now is value. Today, more than ever before, the CIO is positioned perfectly to deliver real value to the business. It is a great time to be an IT leader!

Where Innovation Begins: Understanding the Goals and Objectives of the Business

Many of you know Carol Fawcett as the vice president of global information services at Quest Software. In

September 2012, Quest was acquired by Dell. As a result, Carol is now the CIO at Dell Software. Carol is one of the smartest technology executives I know, and I was honored when she agreed to participate in my new book project.

With more than 70 offices in 23 countries, the company is truly a global organization. In her role, Carol has become an expert juggler of two complementary priorities; business strategy and operational excellence. She also has the distinction of leading the IT organization of a company that employs experienced IT technicians and leaders. For many executives, that alone would be an overwhelming task, but Carol handles it all with incredible grace and equanimity.

My interview with Carol covered a wide range of territory. Here is a brief summary of what she told me:

The key to maintaining the proper balance between strategy and operational excellence is understanding the goals and objectives of the business. If you don't understand the business at all of its levels—from the highest to the lowest—then all the technology in the world is not going to answer the needs of your user base.

You need to understand what your customers need and how the business delivers value to their customers. Only then can you provide the right technology solution and the right innovation.

We always make sure that our people are looking to the future. Our IT organization is not at the bleeding edge, but we've got it tuned up to the point where there's a very thin line between leading and bleeding.

Someone recently asked me how we stay up to date on all the new technologies. I told them that in today's world, there's no excuse for not staying up to date. The Internet makes everything highly visible—you don't have to look very hard to find out what the vendors are doing, you just go their websites.

Or better still, engage in a user community. In many cases, you can learn more from a user community than you can by asking the vendors themselves.

It is also useful going to conferences like the recent CIO Executive Leadership Summit in Palo Alto, because the summit itself is like a walk-in community of IT leaders who are experiencing many of the same exact things you and your team are experiencing.

There are plenty of ways to stay up to date. The information you need is out there—you just need to look for it. And I really believe that most of us in IT would rather do our own research—it's just the way we are built.

Our innovation process is very similar to our overall business strategy. We look at the goals and objectives of the business, and we try to find a winning solution to meet those goals. If the solution is prepackaged, then we might buy it. If it does not exist, then we determine if it is worth building. Our approach to innovation is very business-driven and business-focused. It's never just about innovating for the sake of innovation.

Leading a modern IT organization requires business acumen—you really need to understand the business and you need to know how to communicate with your peers in the business. You have to know how to influence people so they will work well together as a team to achieve the business objectives identified. That's where I believe leadership skills are essential.

I am genuinely impressed by Carol's ability to combine a variety of executive skills into a seamless leadership model. To my mind, Carol exemplifies the twenty-first-century technology executive—a skilled player with a deep understanding of business and a natural sense of balance.

The Four Dimensions of Continuous Innovation and IT Transformation

My good friend Saad Ayub is senior vice president and CIO at Scholastic Inc., one of the world's leading publishers of children's books. The company sells more than 280 million books annually to children in the United States and more than 140 other countries. In addition to its many literary properties, Scholastic is the U.S. distributor of the Harry Potter series, the bestselling children's series of all time. The company also publishes magazines, textbooks, and educational software, and produces children's TV shows.

Keeping track of a global publishing business requires tremendous effort, especially from IT. I think it's fair to say that Scholastic's innovative approach to IT strategy is definitely a major part of the company's ongoing success.

Saad was a panelist at the 2012 CIO Summit of America at the Harvard Club. Here is a brief excerpt of the valuable insights that he shared with the audience:

Generally, when we talk about table stakes, we're talking about how well the IT organization executes. But if you want to talk about bringing innovation to the table, then you need to look at four additional dimensions.

The first dimension is hiring. Is IT hiring people with the right skill sets? Do the people we hire understand cloud, social and mobile computing? Do they have the communication skills required to explain a great idea properly? Do they have the emotional intelligence—the EQ—to follow through successfully? Can they shift their focus from internal to external to leverage trends in fast-moving markets?

The second dimension is the organizational model. The classic IT organization is driven to build and deliver applications. But that does not always address the business challenge. Can we change the organization to shift the focus from delivering applications to delivering business results?

The third dimension is changing our processes. Most of our processes are based around CMMI or ITIL, which brings us back to execution. How do we create processes that allow us to think outside the box, and really innovate for the business?

The fourth dimension is transforming the organization and the process models so that IT can shift its focus from demand management to demand creation. Then you are really positioning IT to help the business drive growth.

I am genuinely impressed with how Saad clearly articulates the four dimensions of change required for true IT transformation and continuous innovation.

Building a Hybrid Platform for Continuous Innovation

When I interview visionary IT thought leaders about continuous innovation, their answers usually fall into two categories. Generally, they tend to believe that innovation results from either a process or a culture.

I respectfully disagree. I believe that effective innovation platforms aren't exclusively "process-driven" or "culture-driven"—they are a hybrid of both.

My friend Peter High describes a continuum for innovation in his book *World Class IT: Why Businesses Succeed When IT Triumphs*.[1] Rather than simply focusing on the steps to innovate, Peter starts with the foundational steps that need to be in place to be able to earn the right to innovate, and to carve enough time from the greater IT department in order to identify new, innovative ideas. Peter's "world class" IT structure includes five principles:

1. People

2. Infrastructure

3. Governance (project and portfolio management)

4. Partnerships with the business

5. External partnerships

Here is what I find particularly interesting about Peter's structure: principles 4 and 5 are where the innovation happens. But you cannot get there unless you have already succeeded at principles 1, 2, and 3.

Essentially, Peter's model aligns with my theory that an innovation platform is neither purely process-driven nor purely culture-driven—it requires both. Moreover, Peter notes that you need to build a great foundation with solid people, reliable, robust, and available infrastructure, and dependable and efficient governance in order to have a real chance to drive innovation.

"Just talking about pursuing innovation isn't going to make it happen," says Peter. "You need to have the first three building-block principles in place. You need great people who can execute. You need an infrastructure that isn't causing headaches, or you'll lose your credibility. You need a governance process that works and delivers projects on time. Now you've got the foundation that enables you to form partnerships, internally with the business and externally with vendors. It's the partnerships that drive meaningful innovation."

If you do these five things well, says Peter, yours will be an IT department that will attract and retain great people, who in turn will develop even better ideas to ensure great performance in the other four principle areas. I like the direction of Peter's thinking for its logic, and also for its practicality.

Making the Case for Top-Down Innovation in the Enterprise

I recently spoke with my good friend John Yapaola, the CEO of Kapow Software in Palo Alto, California. We were talking about the best ways to support innovation within a corporate culture, and John raised a great point: How you innovate depends on the size of the company.

"In a small start-up, where there's very little bureaucracy and everyone is focused on the product, it's easy to innovate on a grassroots level," says John. "In a larger company, grass-roots or bottom-up innovation will be harder, because you're going to crash into the company's traditional ways of doing things. From my perspective, it often makes more sense for the CIO to drive innovation in a big company, because the CIO has the clout and the budget to make it happen."

I really like how John captures the reality of the situation on the ground, and how he puts the focus back on the CIO. John is keenly aware of the challenges facing innovators. As the CEO of a company that provides genuinely innovative solutions to complex software integration problems, he is intimately familiar with the innovation conundrum facing most companies.

I think the best way to express the innovation conundrum is like this: Corporate leadership knows that innovation is a key to success. At the same time, corporate leadership is wary of innovation, because it's extremely difficult to predict the impact of innovation on the status quo (i.e., existing systems and processes).

John says that he is seeing a shift away from purely bottom-up innovation projects and an increasing willingness by CIOs to drive innovation from the IT organization. This shift makes sense for two very good reasons:

1. It enables IT to apply its technical expertise to solving real business problems and delivering value to the enterprise.

2. It reduces the chances of IT being disintermediated by business leaders who believe, rightly or wrongly, that they can deliver innovation faster than IT.

From my perspective, this is all good news. I love hearing that CIOs are stepping up and taking responsibility for driving innovation. I am all in favor of grassroots innovation, but the simple truth is that large companies will always resist, to one degree or another, challenges to the status quo. It is the law of inertia, and that's just the way it is. You can fight it, or you can find a way around it.

Many CIOs, however, are exceptionally well positioned to provide the leadership and expertise required to guide innovation projects through large corporations. I have a feeling that CIO-driven innovation will become the status quo at many large companies. This bodes well for innovation and the IT organization.

Avoiding "the Emperor Has No Clothes" Syndrome

Kendra Bonner is the director of organization effectiveness at Dal-Tile Corporation, the largest ceramic tile manufacturer in the United States and one of the largest tile manufacturers in the world. Prior to joining Dal-Tile, she held similar roles with JCPenney from 2007 to 2011 and Texas Instruments from 2000 to 2006.

With experience working with chief executives across extremely different industries, Kendra has had the opportunity to see what works and what doesn't work when leading transformational change. In a recent conversation about leadership and innovation, she shared her theory on the positive momentum that leaders can harness when they are open to feedback from all levels of the organization.

"A breakdown typically occurs when leaders have created a culture (intentionally or unintentionally) where their direct reports all the way to line workers are afraid to let the emperor know they are naked as a jaybird," says Kendra.

She has seen extremely intelligent leaders miss their targets completely because they dismiss (or never hear) feedback from the ranks, are blinded by their own knowledge, or dismiss the importance of cultural implications for change management.

The greatest ideas truly become great when the entire organization can understand the value they bring and the role they can play in supporting them, and can shape the way in which they are implemented.

"Some of the most effective leaders I have ever worked with are extremely humble, smart enough . . . but not too smart for their own good, open to new ideas and information from all levels of the organization, and they truly care about the people they lead," says Kendra.

Those traits seem to clash with the stereotypical image of strong leadership that we have grown to expect today. People want to be able to relate to their executive leaders and see them as real people, just like them.

When the chasm between the top and bottom ranks seems too wide, it can become impossible to create a culture where information flows freely and honestly to those making the key decisions that drive innovation.

I am delighted that Kendra has added her voice to our conversation. All corporate leaders—including CIOs—should be thinking of ways to enable and support the free flow of knowledge, experience, and insight across the modern enterprise. Ideas can come from anywhere, and we need to have structures and processes in place that can help us turn those ideas into fresh revenue.

Note

1. Peter A. High, *World Class IT: Why Businesses Succeed When IT Triumphs* (San Francisco: Jossey-Bass, 2009).

Chapter 8

Leveraging Social Collaboration to Drive Innovation

In the minds of many CIOs, the term "social collaboration" will always be closely associated with the term "social media," which inevitably evokes thoughts of Facebook, Twitter, Tumblr, and other social networks.

For CIOs, social networks seem inextricably linked to a multitude of tangible business challenges, ranging from security risks to time management issues. As a result, many CIOs tend to approach the whole idea of social collaboration with a certain degree of reluctance.

While this reluctance is quite understandable, it also can be harmful. The overwhelming majority of millennials have grown up with social media. To them, social media feels totally natural—it is an inseparable part of their lives and they aren't going to let go of it anytime soon.

It is not just millennials who are attached to social media. I am going to quote verbatim some key findings from a recent Nielsen report:

- Social networks and blogs continue to dominate Americans' time online, now accounting for nearly a quarter of total time spent on the Internet.

171

- Social media has grown rapidly—today nearly four in five active Internet users visit social networks and blogs.

- Americans spend more time on Facebook than they do on any other U.S. website.

- Close to 40 percent of social media users access social media content from their mobile phone.

- Social networking apps are the third most used among U.S. smartphone owners.

Take a moment to review the top bullet: Nearly 25 percent of the time that Americans use the Internet, they are using social media. To be honest, I think the estimate is probably low. From my perspective, it seems that people under the age of 30 rarely look at e-mail anymore—at least not willingly. Additionally, I would be willing to bet that by the time you read this book, the percentage of social media users accessing social content from mobile devices will have risen dramatically.

Clearly, social media is a trend that we need to acknowledge and address. If we—CIOs and IT leaders—do not provide meaningful solutions, someone else surely will. In one form or another, social technology makes a huge impact on our lives, and I think it makes good business sense to leverage its potential as a force for positive change in the workplace.

Tangible Results Through Social Media

My good friend Mike Barlow is an evangelist for the corporate uses of social collaboration technology. Mike and David B.

Thomas are coauthors of *The Executive's Guide to Enterprise Social Media Strategy*.[1] In the book, they make a good case for seeing social collaboration technology as part of the larger trend of automating business processes across the modern enterprise.

Mike and Dave note that modern corporations tend to be decentralized and increasingly globalized. Since the success of any modern corporation depends heavily on teamwork and collaboration, adopting a technology that enables, improves, and accelerates teamwork and collaboration seems a logical choice.

"Our goal in writing the book was to demonstrate how major corporations like IBM, Accenture, Salesforce.com, Intuit, H&R Block, Newell Rubbermaid, the Mayo Clinic, and SAS leverage the power of social technology to achieve tangible business benefits," says Mike. "We figured out early on [that] many senior executives associate social technology with social networks like Facebook and MySpace, and we wanted to prove that there is a strong business case for using social technology in the modern enterprise."

Mike and Dave argue persuasively that social technology is actually creating a new mode of production in which critical information about changes in markets moves rapidly and efficiently across the enterprise, enabling teams of product developers, engineers, marketers, and salespeople to seize opportunities as they arise, almost in real time.

"In our vision, social technology replaces e-mail as the backbone of internal business communications," says Mike. "Social communication enables and encourages individuals within communities of interest to share their knowledge and information. And remember, this is all taking place behind your firewall."

Here is an example of how this works: Let's say there is an opportunity to sell a new wireless device in Southeast Asia. Someone in the Bangkok office of your company mentions the opportunity in a short status update on your company's internal social collaboration platform. The update is seen by one of your product developers in France. She adds a comment to the update, and alerts your company's head of marketing. The head of marketing adds his comment to the conversation thread and alerts the vice president of manufacturing, who adds a comments and alerts the CFO, who mentions it to the CEO, who alerts the vice president of sales to be ready for a new product launch.

You can see where this is going. Long before your competitors even perceive the opportunity for a new product, your company already has a product in development and is aligning the people and the processes required for bringing it to market.

"We see social collaboration technology as the path toward a new era of incredibly rapid innovation and new product development," says Mike. "We see it as an accelerator that will dramatically increase the speed of business and the introduction of new products in markets all over the world."

Essentially, smart companies will use social collaboration technology to automate innovation and consistently beat their competitors. "Social collaboration is foundational to innovation because it enables and empowers people within the enterprise to share specialized knowledge quickly and effectively," says Mike. "That's the heart of the business case for social collaboration—it accelerates the pace of innovation."

Embracing the Social Workforce

Tony Zingale is the chairman and CEO of Jive Software, the world's leading provider of social business solutions. A pioneer in the software industry, Jive has successfully commercialized social collaboration technology and created enterprise-ready solutions that achieve the goals of improving teamwork, communication, and collaboration in modern companies.

Tony and I spoke recently about the business value of social collaboration technology and its transformational potential. He is passionate in his belief that social collaboration will fundamentally change modern business. Here is a brief summary of what he told me:

> *Businesses have spent billions on hardware, infrastructure, networks, and applications. Collectively, we have successfully automated thousands and thousands of business process.*
>
> *But what have we delivered for the people who actually use those business processes? Yes, we've provided them more network bandwidth, smaller laptops, and smarter phones. But have we delivered what they really need?*

When you ask a roomful of people to name their favorite consumer application, every hand in the room goes up and everyone starts talking. When you ask the same roomful of people to name their favorite business application, no hands go up and the room falls silent.

As an industry, we have not delivered the kind of cool applications that people actually want to use in the workplace, which is the place they're spending anywhere from 40 to 100 hours of their lives every week.

In our personal lives, we have great new technology that's fun to use. In the workplace, we're still using an e-mail system that's 40 years old, an ERP system that's 25 years old, and a CRM [customer relationship management] *application that's 15 years old.*

How can we expect people to achieve their full potential when they're using old tools and old systems? Those older technologies are definitely important, but they're not the whole solution.

Here are the questions that CEOs are asking their CIOs in today's economy: What are best ways to make our workforce more productive? How do we innovate faster and more effectively? How can we do a better job of serving our customers? How do we help our employees, our partners, and our customers become more engaged?

In the past, the answers to those kinds of questions might have involved buying larger databases, acquiring more network capacity, or purchasing more laptops. But today the answers are more complex.

The convergence of cloud, mobile, big data, and social is creating a new paradigm for getting work done. If you read page 1, paragraph 1, sentence 1 of our prospectus when Jive went public at the end of 2011, it says "change the way work gets done." That's our objective—changing the way that people work.

We are part of global trend. Our goal is delivering a work paradigm that is new and different, a work paradigm that takes into account the consumerization of technology and the many new ways in which people actually use technology.

Millennials will grow as a percent of the workforce. We need to embrace the technologies they use, and create business-ready versions of those technologies. That's the future, and that's where business is heading.

I genuinely admire Tony's passion and energy. I firmly believe that his level of intensity is exactly what is needed to elevate the discussion, and to build the foundation for a new workforce paradigm that matches the realities of modern global markets.

Putting Innovation in the Hands of Users

I had a conversation with Gordon Payne recently that I can truly describe as mind-expanding. As many of you already know, Gordon is senior vice president and general manager of the desktop and cloud division at Citrix. He is also a genuinely brilliant guy, and I was delighted to speak with him at length about the future of IT strategy.

From Gordon's perspective, the future is all about user-centricity and mobility. Gordon uses the term "mobile workstyles" to describe the transformative blend of work and personal life that most of us are experiencing right now. For me, the bottom line is that as the boundaries between work and personal life become less certain, CIOs must be ready to adjust IT strategy—especially as new employees who have grown up with the Internet and perceive consumerization as their norm join the company.

In today's hypercompetitive markets, failure to keep pace with user expectations simply poses far too many risks to the enterprise. Internal risks include lost or diminished workforce productivity. External risks include lost or diminished market share, revenue, and profits. Those risks are unacceptable. The good news is that when the enterprise has enlightened IT leadership, those risks are manageable.

My conversation with Gordon was inspiring on many levels. I really appreciate how Gordon sees the mobile workstyle as an evolving condition. Today, it relies on three classes of mobile devices: laptops, tablets, and smartphones. Those devices, in turn, provide three basic technology needs to mobile users: applications, data, and social collaboration.

From the user's point of view, the distinction between devices is less about technology and more about function. All three types of devices can be used to create, consume, and share information, but each type has a distinct specialty. For example, if you need to create a spreadsheet, you will probably boot up your laptop. If you want to read a magazine or watch a movie, you will likely switch on your tablet. And if you want to talk to someone, you will reach into your pocket for your smartphone.

But those distinctions are likely to fade as manufacturers equip their devices with an ever-expanding array of capabilities.

Again, the bottom line is that IT cannot sit still and wait for the next game-changing device to emerge. IT will have to get out in front of the curve, develop a list of likely scenarios, and start planning before users switch to the next big thing and IT is left scrambling to accommodate a new set of needs.

In the old days, waiting for the tide to turn seemed like an acceptable IT management strategy. IT needs to use its expertise and its deep knowledge of technology to anticipate the next wave and be ready when it hits the beach.

Now is the time to experiment with cloud, mobile, and social technologies. Waiting is not a strategy—the storm will come whether you are prepared or not. This is the beginning of an epic revolution, and it is your choice to join or watch from the sidelines.

As it turns out, Citrix is not waiting. Just after our conversation, Citrix announced the acquisition of Podio, a software-as-a-service collaborative work platform. Podio enables users and teams to collaborate in real time, and adds the ability for any user to create their own preferred workflow. Collaboration platforms put opportunities for innovation in the hands of the users, which is certainly a step in the right direction.

Innovation and Social Collaboration

Whitney Bouck, a close colleague of mine, is general manager of Enterprise at Box, the leading cloud content-sharing and collaboration solution. Whitney is responsible for driving the growth strategy for Box in the enterprise market, which gives her a unique perspective on the intersection of cloud and innovation in modern global business.

Box is based in Los Altos—the heart of Silicon Valley—and is backed by venture capital firms Andreessen Horowitz, Bessemer Venture Partners, Draper Fisher Jurvetson, Emergence Capital Partners, General Atlantic, Meritech Capital Partners, NEA, Scale Venture Partners, and U.S. Venture Partners. The company's mission is straightforward: make it simple for people to manage information and collaborate effectively from anywhere on any device, while providing IT the visibility and control that make it a sound solution for business.

I firmly believe that seamless collaboration among teams and individuals—across the enterprise and beyond its traditional boundaries—is a critical competitive advantage in today's incredibly fast-moving markets. The capability for supporting friction-free collaboration is also absolutely foundational if your goal is building a culture of continuous and sustained innovation.

Innovative companies such as Box make it possible for organizations to innovate on a routine basis. And the same technology provides visibility into the use and flow of content, which enables smart companies to optimize the collaborative processes that result in continuous innovation and market leadership.

Three years ago, this kind of talk might have sounded like hype. But that is no longer the case. Today, industry leaders such as P&G, McAfee, Nationwide, and Red Bull use Box technology to support and enable the global collaboration strategies that are essential to their success.

"This is very exciting, because we're changing the way that people are working," says Whitney. "We're shifting the workflow from e-mail to the cloud, which enables global teams to work together on projects, no matter where they are. Taking the workflow out of e-mail and putting it into the cloud creates amazing new efficiencies and greatly accelerates collaboration across the enterprise and beyond."

Instead of sending large files through FTP servers, teams and individuals can share them with authorized users anywhere in the world. And the best part is that the dialogues and conversation threads become part of the shared knowledge base. You just cannot do that with e-mail.

The rapid growth of Box, which was founded in 2005, is a sure sign of the times. Companies now understand why knowledge sharing, collaboration, and innovation are crucial for success in competitive markets.

"When I started, we had 150 employees. Now we have more than 600. We have 14 million individuals and 140,000 businesses that use Box to discover information, connect with collaborators, and engage with content. It's very exciting," says Whitney. "Enterprise cloud collaboration is transforming and enhancing business at every link in the global value chain."

Note

1. Mike Barlow and David B. Thomas, *The Executive's Guide to Enterprise Social Media Strategy: How Social Networks Are Radically Transforming Your Business* (Hoboken, NJ: John Wiley & Sons, 2011).

Chapter 9

Living with Uncertainty

A dozen of the nation's top CIOs had the opportunity recently to spend several hours of quality time with Dr. William LaFontaine, vice president of strategy and worldwide operations at IBM. Bill is one of Big Blue's most respected thought leaders, and he agreed to brief the CIOs on IBM's 2012 Global Technology Outlook (GTO), a special report on the trends most likely to create both disruptions and business opportunities in the near term.

Bill's audience for the briefing was the HMG Strategy CIO Executive Leadership Alliance (CELA), a select group of C-level technology execs who meet regularly to share their knowledge and experience. The briefing was held at the IBM Industry Solutions Lab at the T. J. Watson Research Center in Hawthorne, New York.

I moderated the lively roundtable discussion that accompanied the briefing. And though our confidentiality agreement with IBM precludes me from sharing precise details of

Bill's presentation, I can offer you edited highlights of the report's findings:

- **Managing uncertain data at scale.** Making revolutionary use of big data and analytics and managing uncertainty at scale.

- **Systems of people.** Leveraging social business to address workforce pain points through analytics and capture insights about the way people work.

- **Outcome-based business.** Transforming IT from cost containment to business value.

- **Resilient business and services.** Heightened need for resiliency in light of globalization and consolidation trends, which increase enterprise exposure to natural disasters and cyber-attacks.

- **Future of analytics.** Explosion of unstructured data amplifies need for development platforms and systems to support the scale and modalities of emerging analytics.

- **The future Watson.** Moving beyond simple "question-in and answer-out" to evidence-based decision support with interactive dialogue and continuous learning.

Now you know what is keeping senior executives at IBM awake at night!

The objective of the Global Technology Outlook is straightforward: to identify significant technology trends that can potentially create new businesses.

The two dominant themes of the GTO are analytics and data. The report focuses specifically, however, on the multiple challenges presented by the explosive growth of unstructured and uncertain data. As Bill mentioned in his briefing, 80 percent of available data will be unstructured and uncertain in 2015, compared to 30 percent today. That trend will present monumental challenges to CIOs over the next couple of years. The bottom line is that if you think it is hard to manage terabytes and exobytes of *structured* data, imagine the difficulties of managing even larger quantities of *unstructured* data!

These kinds of challenges will accelerate the need for newer, better, and faster analytics and solutions designed specifically for handling big data.

As most of you already know, one of the biggest drivers of unstructured data is social media. Bill made a great case for viewing modern corporations as "systems of people" in which real value is created by the daily interactions of people. The hard part, of course, is mapping and mining the mountains of data generated by those interactions, and then presenting it in a way that's genuinely meaningful to the business.

I love the way Bill framed the challenge of leveraging social data: "Optimizing people-centric processes is *not* the same as optimizing supply chains." That being said, the opportunities suggested by mining social data are huge. Imagine using real-time social data to optimize sales force productivity, improve the ROI of marketing processes, or create new products on the fly. The potential rewards would be enormous.

It is always a thrill to visit the IBM Industry Solutions Lab—we even had a chance to meet Watson, the world's smartest computer, and play a quick round of Jeopardy!

Keep Your Eyes on the B2B Internet

Conversations today about e-commerce and Web 2.0 tend to focus more on business-to-consumer (B2C) models than on business-to-business (B2B) models. That focus is about to shift, mostly due to the swift adoption of cloud-based service delivery models that make it far easier for companies to conduct complex, large-scale business processes and transactions over the Internet—without sacrificing confidentiality and security.

Until a better term is coined, I am calling this phenomenon the "B2B Internet." It is definitely a significant component of the epic revolution that's transforming business and commerce all over the world.

Innovative firms such as Okta, the market-leading on-demand identity and access management service, are fueling the growth of the B2B Internet by enabling companies to accelerate the secure adoption of their Web-based applications, both in the cloud and behind the firewall.

This trend creates tremendous opportunities for CIOs and other IT leaders, since it allows them to create robust and highly secure architectures for sharing and exchanging critical business information across every link of the supply chain.

I had a great conversation recently about the growth of the Internet's B2B side with Todd McKinnon, Okta's CEO and cofounder. Todd rightly notes that the B2B trend is driven by the incredibly rapid adoption of cloud and mobile technologies.

"Companies that build truly collaborative applications across the supply chain will gain huge advantages in their markets," he says. "Smart CIOs will harness cloud and mobile to establish new types of networks that will enable their companies to connect more closely and more seamlessly with suppliers and customers. That ability to connect will make a big difference."

There is no question that the appeal of cloud and mobile has forced many CIOs to rethink their earlier opposition and embrace them as parts of the new reality. Todd's mission at Okta is making it easier for those CIOs to leverage the potential of cloud and mobile technologies, while safeguarding existing IT assets.

We spoke about an article that Todd had written recently for *Fast Company*, in which he cited the need for a more nuanced approach to IT leadership in times of major change and transformation.

"For me personally, I've found you need to be a little more aggressive when you're in a situation where a major change is required," says Todd. "If you're just looking for incremental improvements, if you're just tweaking and nudging, then it's okay to be less aggressive. But when you really need to move the needle, then you have to adjust your leadership style. You can't just take incremental bites, you need to be bold."

This is sound advice. There are many styles of leadership, and some are more appropriate in certain situations than in others. The hard part is deciding which style of leadership is right for the situation, and which style is right for you and your organization.

Trust, Freedom, and Responsibility: Keys to Transformational Leadership and Continuous Innovation

I had a truly inspiring conversation recently with Mike Kail, vice president of IT operations at Netflix. Mike's perspectives on innovation and leadership are incredibly valuable, and I want to share them with you.

Netflix is a great example of a company that's leaning forward and embracing new technology as a competitive advantage. The company recently migrated from a traditional enterprise finance platform to a cloud-based solution from Workday. The decision to switch from the classic platform to a relatively new, off-premise solution captures the innovative spirit of the Netflix team.

"We're taking a bleeding-edge approach to replacing custom on-premise legacy enterprise software applications with cloud-based alternatives," says Mike. "We're enabling the IT team to focus on delivering results instead of focusing on bolting together infrastructure and maintaining a bunch of custom software."

I love where Mike is going with this. He sees the cloud as a logical alternative for classic IT operations, and he is moving aggressively to reduce complexity across the IT portfolio.

Mike's ability to pursue a genuinely transformational IT strategy is based on trust—the C-suite relies on his judgment and his knowledge. At Netflix, trust is embedded into the corporate culture, and it enables Mike and his colleagues to move much more quickly than their counterparts at more traditional companies.

"We have developed a culture that embraces freedom and responsibility," Mike explains. "We hire intelligent, fully formed adults and then we allow them to do their jobs without encumbering them with processes that exist just for the sake of having processes. For example, if I want to move a service into the cloud, I don't have to get a sign-off from our CEO or sit in a meeting with our CFO and explain every detail. They trust me to make the right choices and to take responsibility for making it work. That is a big part of how we can move more quickly than the competition."

When I listen to Mike, I hear the future of IT. It is a future in which IT leaders are given the freedom and the responsibility to make the best decisions for their companies, a future in which CIOs have more than a "seat at the table"—they are trusted members of the executive leadership team.

At Netflix, words like freedom, trust, and responsibility are not used lightly. They define the culture. Reed Hastings, the company's CEO, lists nine behaviors and skills that are highly valued at Netflix: judgment, communication, impact, curiosity, innovation, courage, passion, honesty, and selflessness. Those qualities are encouraged, supported, and rewarded across the Netflix corporate culture.

When Mike hires new staff for the IT team, he looks at more than the applicant's technical abilities. He also considers how well they understand the culture. "We probably put as much, if not more, emphasis on the cultural fit. Working here requires more than being smart. It requires the ability to work in a high-performance culture of innovation."

Key Traits of Innovative IT Leaders

My friend Puneet Bhasin is senior vice president and CIO at Waste Management, Inc. From his office in Houston, he has a unique view of how the innovation process works at a company that serves nearly 20 million municipal, commercial, industrial, and residential customers through a network of 367 collection operations, 355 transfer stations, 273 active landfill disposal sites, 16 waste-to-energy plants, 104 recycling plants, and 111 beneficial-use landfill gas projects.

I had the opportunity to chat with Puneet recently, and I asked him to describe the attributes of an innovative IT leader. Here is a brief summary of his response:

IT leaders need three key traits to be successful innovators. First, you need an intimate understanding of the business strategy and the levers that move that business strategy in a positive direction. You need the ability to marry and mesh IT initiatives with the business strategy. People ask me, "What's your IT strategy?" I proudly say, "I don't have one." I really don't. But I do have a business strategy. To me, IT strategy is a set of initiatives that are designed to achieve a business strategy.

The second thing you need is an intimate understanding of your customers and of your operations. I always advise my people to spend time with the customers, visit their locations, ride the trucks, go to a landfill, sit down at a call center, listen in to calls, go with the salespersons. Find out what our competitors are doing. Develop an in-depth understanding of the business, the customers, and the marketplace.

The third thing, which is the hardest, is using your creative juices to envision innovative solutions using technology to achieve the objectives of the business. That's an innate skill. It can be tough to learn. It's all about thinking out of the box, questioning the status quo, coming up with ideas that are always optimizing, and tweaking and enhancing what you do.

A lot of people think that innovation is all about using some new technology that nobody has thought of before. To me, innovation is about using a standard technology in a nonstandard way, as opposed to using a nonstandard technology in a standard way.

I really like how Puneet sees innovation as a practical process. It's clear that his perspective has been shaped by his experiences as an IT leader in several industries. Prior to joining WM, he was a senior vice president and chief information officer for Monster Worldwide. Before that, he was a senior vice president at Putnam Investments, and CIO at Greenlight.com and Ryder TRS.

Innovation should be a company-wide effort, according to Puneet. Here is what he told me:

I personally have tried many different innovation models. I have created dedicated innovation groups within my department. I have created special environments with the latest equipment to help teams innovate faster. I have set aside "innovation days" in which people can present their innovative ideas. I have experimented with the Google model, in which you dedicate a certain percent of somebody's time purely to innovation.

None of those models have worked for me. What has worked for me is having a culture of innovation. What is a culture of innovation? It is a culture that is open to different ideas, questions the status quo, and rewards people for innovative thinking. It's a culture that continuously develops new ways for using technology to open up new markets and improve the way we serve our customers.

From my perspective, having an overall culture of innovation is more helpful than setting up a special group or department. When everyone feels empowered to innovate, great things happen.

Security Is Integral to IT Strategy

I had a great conversation recently with Patricia Titus, the chief information security officer at Symantec. Prior to joining Symantec, she was vice president and global chief information security officer (CISO) for Unisys Corporation. Before that, she was CISO at the Transportation Security Administration within the Department of Homeland Security. She has also worked overseas for several years in various positions within the U.S. Department of Defense, the U.S. State Department, and various private-sector firms.

In all, she has more than 20 years of security management experience. When Patricia talks about IT security, I listen closely. One of the topics we discussed was the need for security that's tightly integrated into the IT architecture, as opposed to bolted on as an afterthought.

"We need to move past the old mindsets and look at security from a holistic perspective," says Patricia. "In the modern global economy, companies increasingly need integrated, end-to-end solutions that address the challenges created by mobility, cloud, and big data."

The good news is that the rapid growth of cloud and mobile is creating more opportunities for integrating security up-front and organically. In the old mindset, security was often an afterthought. In the new mindset described by Patricia, security is integrated from the beginning.

"The newer technologies actually give us the chance to build security into the platform baseline," she says.

The idea of building security into the platform, as opposed to adding it later, is important, because security has a direct impact on the CIO's effectiveness as a corporate officer. Patricia estimates that modern CIOs spend "30 to 40 percent of their time" dealing directly or indirectly with security issues. That represents a huge chunk of the day, especially when you consider that most of the remaining time is devoted to operational issues.

When you spend a third of your day worrying about security and the rest of it dealing with operations, it does not leave you much for the kind of creativity required to drive innovation and create real value across the enterprise.

That is why I think it is important to consider Patricia's advice to look at security from a holistic perspective. An enterprise-wide strategy will probably be more effective than a series of point solutions, and the net impact will be to reduce the overall amount of time and energy you devote to security issues. Then you can redirect that time and energy toward projects and activities that will help the company achieve its business goals.

Maintaining Credibility: You Have to Know When to Get Down in the Weeds

Michelle Garvey is the CIO of ANN INC., one of the leading specialty retailers for fashionable women's clothing. In many ways, ANN INC. embodies the successful twenty-first-century retailer, combining traditional bricks-and-mortar stores with robust e-commerce operations. The company's Ann Taylor and LOFT brands are marketed in nearly 1,000 stores in

46 states, the District of Columbia, and Puerto Rico through four channels: Ann Taylor stores, LOFT stores, Ann Taylor Factory, and LOFT Outlet. They are also available online at www.anntaylor.com and www.loft.com.

Modern retailers such as ANN INC. offer a steady stream of challenges and opportunities for CIOs and IT leaders. But you need a deep reservoir of credibility and trust so you can take advantage of opportunities when they arise.

The best way to build credibility and trust is through flawless execution. But in the real world, things go wrong. The mark of a true leader is the ability to deal with problems honestly and effectively.

"Before you are accepted as a strategic partner, you have to be perceived as a good manager," says Michelle. "You need to be aligned with goals and objectives of the business. You have to earn your credibility and earn your right to be at the table."

When problems arise, as they invariably do, you need to be thoroughly engaged in the problem-solving process. "You need an intuitive grasp of when to get down in the weeds. People won't always ask for help. They will try to fix their own problems, even when they're in over their head. It's human nature. But as the leader, you need to know when to step in and be proactive."

You also need to be absolutely honest and transparent when something goes wrong. And you need to demonstrate your involvement—show people that you care and that you're willing to spend your time solving the problem.

"Every problem has three tracks leading toward a solution," says Michelle. "The first track is determining what happened and make it stop happening. The second track is finding out if data or information has been damaged, and then doing whatever is necessary to get the data accurate and complete. The third track is figuring out what went wrong in the first place. Was it a failure of governance? Was it caused by schedule pressure? How do you address the problem on a go-forward basis? If you are open with your process and share it with the people who were adversely affected, you will build credibility and trust."

Michelle also raised a related point that I want to share with you: Flagging a problem is not the same as solving a problem.

"In some organizations, there's almost a belief that identifying a risk is the same as mitigating it. People sometimes think that by discussing a risk, they're preventing it. That's obviously not the case, but I've seen it happen," she says.

The CIO can help the company avoid that type of scenario, Michelle says, by thoroughly explaining the potential impact and likelihood of the risk, and then taking the appropriate action to mitigate the risk and agree on contingency/remediation plans if the risk comes to pass.

"You have to help people understand the impact of the risk, and then you need to be proactive about slowing, rescheduling, or stopping the project that is generating the risk," she says.

I also asked Michelle about to comment briefly about the future of IT. As an experienced CIO, she does not see the role of IT diminishing.

"I don't see IT getting smaller, but I do see it shifting its emphasis," she says. "If you look back at the history of IT, you can see that we have a lot fewer tape librarians now than we had in the past. We have fewer people mounting hard disks on spindles and fewer people doing data entry."

The IT function is evolving from the relatively clear-cut role of pure technology enablement to a significantly more complex role that includes diverse and overlapping functions such as product development, intellectual property, sales, marketing, supply chain management, finance, business process optimization, and customer satisfaction.

"The future of IT is all about understanding what the technology is capable of doing and understanding how that technology can help the business," says Michelle. "That's the new sweet spot."

Think Multiregional Before Committing to Global Markets

I write and speak frequently about the need for IT leaders to become more proactively involved in helping their firms identify and enter new markets. Sometimes I use the term "global markets" to suggest the broader range of possibilities that exist outside of traditional domestic markets.

My friend David Smith reminded me recently that what looks like a global market from one perspective can look like a regional market from another perspective. David is chief executive and cofounder of Global Futures and Foresight, a strategic futures think tank based in the United Kingdom. One of his specialties is surveying the differences between markets, so his comments are particularly relevant. Here is a brief summary of what David told me in our conversation:

Many people talk about global strategy. But there's also a real need for multiregional strategies, where you take regional differences into account. For example, Asia-Pacific is made up of many regions with various languages, cultures, economies, social norms, topographies, and infrastructures. So you really can't have a global strategy for Asia-Pacific. You need a multiregional strategy for Asia-Pacific.

The CIO can help the business develop a multiregional strategy by spending time in the regions and getting a firsthand look at what's happening on the ground. CIOs need to know about the region's IT infrastructure. In some parts of the world, the infrastructure is highly developed. In other parts, it might be nonexistent.

End-user devices can also pose challenges for "global" IT strategies. Devices that might be perfectly appropriate for most of Europe might be inappropriate for rural parts of China or India.

The bottom line is that you've got to find out for your-self. Different cultures have different ways of using social tools, which creates different patterns of collaboration. Again, you have to know the differences so you don't waste time and money buying equipment or systems that will be underutilized.

The good news is that newer mobile technologies are making it easier for more people to access IT resources from wherever they are. We've entered a new age of truly globalized communications, and that's genuinely exciting. What we need is more understanding of the many regional markets that make up the global market that everyone talks about.

I really like David's nuanced perspective on globalization and the need for multiregional strategies. It seems logical to me that when you want to go global, you have to start local—even when "local" means somewhere on the other side of the world!

Walking the Talk

Recently, I was extremely fortunate to catch up with my good friend Sheila Jordan. Sheila is vice president of communication and collaboration IT at Cisco, the global leader in networking. Her responsibilities include Cisco .com (the company's external website), enterprise content management, communication and collaboration solutions, CEC (Cisco's internal website), internal deployment of Cisco's TelePresence technology, and IT support for HR, finance, marketing, and emerging technology deployment.

Sheila's prime focus is the delivery of a communication and collaboration platform that combines the power of new technologies with applications, services, and business processes to deliver greater productivity, growth, and innovation across Cisco. In addition, she is responsible for the transformation of the customer experience on Cisco .com, which utilizes new technologies to create stronger relationships with customers through collaboration.

It is fair to say that Sheila plays a key leadership role in Cisco's innovation strategy. We spoke for about an hour about the intersection of innovation and leadership in modern global corporations. Here is a very brief summary of what she told me:

Some people think that innovation is all about inventing bright new shiny objects. To me, innovation is also about simplifying processes, reducing complexity, and making it easier for people to accomplish their tasks. It's very hard to take something that's complex and make it simple—but that's where innovation can really help the organization and help the customer.

This year, I have a list of 12 objectives. Not one of those objectives mentions "innovation" by name, but it will take innovation to accomplish most of them.

In the past, many people thought that you needed a special department or special team to innovate. Today, we understand that you need to embed innovation in what you're doing on a regular basis.

Top executives can set the tone, but the innovation itself should come from every level in the organization. When everyone feels empowered to be an innovator, you get innovation across the enterprise.

I think that Sheila really hits the target when she describes an enterprise-wide innovation strategy. In today's fast-moving world, it doesn't make sense to entrust innovation to a small team locked in an ivory tower. You really need input from everyone in the organization—because you never know when someone will come up with a great idea that enables the company to open new markets and win new customers.

For Many Reasons, Now Is the Perfect Time to Be the CIO

I spoke recently with my friend Jim Knight, executive vice president and global CIO at the Chubb Group of Insurance Companies, the nation's eleventh largest property and casualty insurer. Chubb's roots as a company extend 125 years into the past, but when Jim and I spoke, we focused on the future. From Jim's perspective, the future is more than just bright—it is brilliant!

"Moore's Law is still in effect and the cost of technology continues to drop," says Jim. "When you factor in trends such as miniaturization, consumerization, cloud, mobile, and social, you can see that we're in the midst of a revolution that is unlike any revolution of the past. This revolution is feeding itself—and it's going to keep on going for a long time."

The incredibly swift pace of change and transformation puts the CIO in a truly unique position. In a continuing technology revolution, the knowledge, expertise, and experience of the CIO and the IT team can bring incalculable value to the enterprise.

"Fifteen years ago, you could ask someone to describe what technology would look like three years in the future," says Jim. "Today, you just can't look that far ahead. You cannot predict with any reasonable accuracy what will be happening three years from now."

That being said, there's plenty of opportunity on the horizon. "There are lots of trees out there with fruit that's ready to be picked, and lots of trees with fruit that still ripening," says Jim. "This is a gift that keeps giving."

But you have to know which opportunities are ready for harvesting. That's where the CIO's knowledge can be invaluable. Some technologies can provide temporary advantages, while others can offer long-term benefits. Chubb, for example, is using advanced data analytics to create new value from its extensive database. "Applying some of the newer analytics to our data creates a unique advantage for us in the market," says Jim. "This is something that our competitors cannot do because they don't have the kind of data that we have."

I especially like how Jim envisions the future as a place of boundless opportunity and how he sees the role of the CIO becoming even more relevant as information technology continues advancing. It certainly makes sense to me that as the technology becomes more complex, powerful, and sophisticated, companies will need senior-level executives who understand the opportunities and benefits of forward-looking IT strategies. That's why I echo Jim's sentiment that now is the perfect time to be a CIO.

Revisiting the Relationship Between Innovation and Entrepreneurship

Earlier in this book, I briefly quoted Bruce Rosenstein, the managing editor of *Leader to Leader* and the author of *Living in More Than One World: How Peter Drucker's Wisdom Can Inspire and Transform Your Life*.[1] Since Bruce is an authority on the subject, I asked him how Drucker would have viewed the challenges and opportunities of innovation strategy. Here are my questions, followed by Bruce's responses:

Based on your understanding of Peter Drucker's philosophy and worldview, how would he have characterized the importance of innovation as part of an enterprise growth strategy?

The world is a different place from when he died in 2005, especially because of social media, advances in technology, and the drastically changed economy. But I think the beauty of his principles is that many are timeless and can be applied no matter what changes we have seen in technology, society, and business. He thought that innovation was an economic or social term, not a technical one.

Drucker believed that growth is a necessity to meet the demands of the future. He believed companies should grow better, even if they did not grow bigger. And if they grew to a particular size, they were candidates for reorganization. Innovation is important because it helps a company create tomorrow on its own terms.

Some companies seem stuck between the idea of having an innovation process and an innovation culture. Which concept would Drucker have championed?

A company needs a variety of processes (that will probably change over time) to deal with innovation and to manage change. Yet Drucker also believed that unless a company maintains an atmosphere conducive to innovation (whether or not it is called an innovation culture), then these processes will tend to be hit-or-miss. Innovation must be purposeful, forward-looking, and requires lots of hard work and perseverance before reaching its potential. He was a holistic systems thinker, and recommended that processes of change require a thorough understanding of a company's complete current realities. There is a wonderful quote from his 1993 book The Ecological Vision *that really speaks to this idea of culture, without using the terminology: "I came to realize that the only way in which an institution, whether a government, a university, a business, a labor union, an army, can maintain continuity is by building systematic, organized innovation into its very structure." Drucker's influential 1985 book* Innovation and Entrepreneurship: Principles and Practices *is must reading for anyone who is serious about these* topics. *Although some of the examples are dated, it is still vibrant and is often referenced by current management/ leadership authors.*

What's the best way of describing Drucker's view on the relationship between innovation and entrepreneurship?

Both innovation and entrepreneurship focus on new ways of achieving success and making a difference. Drucker describes entrepreneurship as "the institution that is the carrier of innovation."

Both are concerned with the creation of not only products and services, but of new ways of doing things, even the creation of new industries, and in entrepreneurship, creating new businesses or other institutions. But he was careful to note that neither were matters of waiting for the muse and a "flash of genius." Both require hard work, possibly over a long period of time.

In other words, you don't even necessarily have to think of yourself as a creative person to be innovative or entrepreneurial. You just need to be able to put in the right sort of work in however long it takes. Both also require a certain amount of letting go of the present and the past, one of his favorite themes. He called it both planned or systematic abandonment.

It requires asking yourself, "If we were not doing this already, knowing what we know now, would we start now?" If the answer was no, as he often found to be the case, he believed that action was required, not more thought and analysis. He also acknowledged that this was easier said

than done, especially since people put so much misplaced
energy into defending yesterday.

Innovation and entrepreneurship tap into very similar
thought processes. This means that we don't necessarily
need to be talking about creating a new business or new
product lines. Social innovation is also highly important.
Drucker wrote about the emergence of the megachurch
phenomenon of the past 30 years. The innovative and
entrepreneurial leaders of these churches (such as Drucker's
longtime friend Rick Warren of Saddleback Church, author
of The Purpose-Driven Life*) figured out new ways to serve*
people in radically different types of churches, especially
by reaching out to people who were not affiliated with a
church, and involving them in considerably different
ways from other religious institutions. Membership in
Saddleback and many others started quite small and grew
to many thousands of parishioners.

When Drucker writes of innovating for the present (as
opposed to innovating for the future), what did he mean?
Why is it important to differentiate between present and
future innovation?

He felt that since the future could not be predicted, it was
better to innovate for the relatively near term, when you
could at least have an idea if a market existed or could
be created. And you would have to take into account the
time span from deciding on an innovation and bringing
it to market. In another sense, a radical innovation may
mean almost a complete break from the present, while
more incremental innovation would take place more

within the present business. This would happen when the innovation represented continuous improvement of a process or product.

I think it's also important to remember that Drucker defined innovation in different ways at different times. These definitions included such themes as creating new value and new ways of satisfying customers, applying existing knowledge to create new knowledge, and improving the yields of existing resources, which would speak to the idea of innovating for the present.

Yet even this type of innovation has implications for the future, if only to provide a new baseline for future performance or to eventually phase out a product or service for something new. The key thing is that Drucker was always thinking about the future, and how companies and individuals could make the future, rather than just react to it, or be blindsided by it. His long-standing phrase was "the future that has already happened," referring to the predictable effects of events that have taken place that will have implications for a business or other institutions.

Drucker emphasizes the importance of keeping innovations simple and tightly focused. Why does he make that point, and what experiences led him to that belief?

He was concerned that companies should work on innovations that were well thought out in terms of market possibilities, customer satisfaction, and problems they might solve. If you were not focused, your attention and resources would be scattered and less effective. It would be too difficult to communicate and explain to other people in your company, who have to understand what you're attempting to accomplish. Innovations also required the right people working on them and their own budget.

He also warned to be on the lookout for the unexpected success. The market for your new product or service might be different from the one you envisioned. Don't shut the door on future success because the result you achieved doesn't look like what you expected during your planning.

The Emerging Ecosystem of Continuous Innovation and Transformation

Apple, Amazon, Google, Facebook, Salesforce.com, Boeing, and eBay are among the acknowledged leaders in innovation. The results of their innovations are experienced daily by billions of people all over the world.

With such striking examples of success right in front of us, it's fair to ask: Why aren't all companies innovating? Or maybe the right question is this: What *prevents* companies from innovating?

My research and investigation into these questions led me to this comparison: Innovation is a lot like playing the piano. You need to master several different skills and then apply them at just the right time. By themselves, none of the skills are really difficult—the hard part is putting them together in the right order and at the right moment.

My research also turned up another interesting item: Innovative market leaders seem to intuitively grasp the complex and incredibly powerful connection between innovation, social media, cloud computing, and big data.

In other words, the market leaders aren't innovating in a vacuum. They are innovating within an *innovation ecosystem* and leveraging the most powerful tools to achieve spectacular results.

I realized that very few people genuinely understand how innovation occurs, how it can be encouraged, and how it can become part of an organization's cultural DNA.

It took me a while to fully grasp just how little is generally understood about the multiple processes required to generate innovation and about the complex relationships among innovation, transformation, and continuous improvement.

I think it is fair to say that the average person has a fairly mysterious notion of what innovation is, why it is increasingly critical to the health of competitive organizations, how it takes place, and who does it. Ask the average person to describe innovation and you're likely to get a murky answer.

Clearly, we need to remove the mystery. It is okay for the average person to have a tenuous understanding of how innovation works. But in today's hypercompetitive markets, it is imperative for senior corporate officers to develop a deep understanding of how innovation works and how a culture of continuous innovation can be created.

I believe that within the next three years, innovation will be commonly perceived as a core competency. The idea that "some companies innovate and some" don't will fall away, and there will be a general agreement that innovation is an absolutely critical piece of corporate strategy. More companies will hire chief innovation officers, and more resources will be committed to supporting innovation.

I think we are at the dawn of an exciting new era. I think we are witnessing the beginning of our generation's greatest leap forward.

I am confident that CIOs and senior technology executives will play major leadership roles in this exciting new era of innovation, collaboration, and continuous transformation. I genuinely look forward to the global conversation that will emerge as we move forward to create our shared future.

A Historic Moment

The convergence of mobile, social, and cloud computing has created an historic moment for the modern CIO. Ubiquitous communication, new social norms, and a broad portfolio of powerful digital assets are creating a new world of opportunity and risk.

Modern organizations will look to their CIOs for guidance, expertise, and counsel in this new landscape. CEOs will expect CIOs to provide the leadership, innovation, and transformation required to stay ahead of the competition in rapidly changing markets.

The opportunity is truly monumental. And so are the risks. Are you prepared? Are you ready to take your game to the next level?

The high velocity of change is forcing CIOs to act more boldly. This represents a sharp break with tradition, but there's really no other viable choice. CIOs can step up and embrace the challenges of the new marketplace. Or they can face the consequences.

Companies that have embraced the potential of the new economy are flourishing. Innovative companies such as Salesforce.com, IBM, VMware, Box, Workday, and Boeing have leveraged the knowledge and experience of their IT assets to open new markets and reach new customers with fantastic new products—at a fraction of the time and cost that would have been required a mere 18 months ago!

This is not just a trend—it is a tectonic shift from past practices. The implications are genuinely amazing in scope, for CIOs and the companies they serve.

Do you have the skills to ride this wave? Are you prepared to offer the leadership required to maintain a culture of continuous innovation and transformation? Will you be an evangelist for technology? Will you bring real value to the table?

CIOs have the perfect vantage point from which to see all aspects of the enterprise. CIOs have the perspective, the experience and the knowledge to offer constructive leadership that enriches the business. My hope is that 2013–2014 will be remembered as the Year of the CIO.

As a community, we have a responsibility to lead. I am confident that we can exceed the expectations, and raise the bar significantly for the next generation of IT leaders.

Let me leave you with an inspiring piece of writing from Walter Isaacson's biography of Steve Jobs.[2] The passage appears toward the end of the book, when Isaacson is summing up Steve's legacy:

Was he smart? No, not exceptionally. Instead he was a genius. His imaginative leaps were instinctive, unexpected, and at times magical. . . . Like a pathfinder, he could absorb information, sniff the winds, and sense what lay ahead.

Steve Jobs thus became the greatest business executive of our era, the one most certain to be remembered a century from now.

Notes

1. Bruce Rosenstein, *Living in More Than One World: How Peter Drucker's Wisdom Can Inspire and Transform Your Life* (San Francisco: Berrett-Koehler, 2009).

2. Walter Isaacson, *Steve Jobs* (New York: Simon & Schuster, 2011).

RECOMMENDED READING

Adams, James L. *Conceptual Blockbusting: A Guide to Better Ideas*. 4th ed. New York: Basic Books, 2001.

Barlow, Mike, and David B. Thomas. *The Executive's Guide to Enterprise Social Media Strategy: How Social Networks Are Radically Transforming Your Business*. Hoboken, NJ: John Wiley & Sons, 2011.

Berkun, Scott. *The Myths of Innovation*. Sebastopol, CA: O'Reilly Media, 2010.

Carr, Nicholas. *The Big Switch: Rewiring the World, from Edison to Google*. New York: W. W. Norton, 2008.

Christensen, Clayton M. *The Innovator's Dilemma: The Revolutionary Book That Will Change the Way You Do Business*. New York: HarperBusiness, 2000.

Christensen, Clayton M., and Michael E. Raynor. *The Innovator's Solution: Creating and Sustaining Successful Growth*. Boston: Harvard Business Review Press, 2003.

Collins, Jim. *Good to Great: Why Some Companies Make the Leap . . . and Others Don't*. New York: HarperCollins, 2001.

Diamandis, Peter H., and Steven Kotler. *Abundance: The Future Is Better Than You Think*. New York: Free Press, 2012.

Drucker, Peter. *Innovation and Entrepreneurship*. New York: Harper & Row, 1985.

Duhigg, Charles. *The Power of Habit: Why We Do What We Do in Life and Business*. New York: Random House, 2012.

Dyer, Jeff, Hal Gregersen, and Clayton M. Christensen. *The Innovator's DNA: Mastering the Five Skills of Disruptive Innovators*. Boston: Harvard Business Review Press, 2011.

Gladwell, Malcolm. *Outliers: The Story of Success*. New York: Little, Brown, 2008.

Gross, Daniel. *Better, Stronger, Faster: The Myth of American Decline and the Rise of a New Economy*. New York: Free Press, 2012.

Hamel, Gary. *What Matters Now: How to Win in a World of Relentless Change, Ferocious Competition, and Unstoppable Innovation*. San Francisco: Jossey-Bass, 2012.

Heath, Chip, and Dan Heath. *Made to Stick: Why Some Ideas Survive and Others Die*. New York: Random House, 2007.

Isaacson, Walter. *Steve Jobs*. New York: Simon & Schuster, 2011.

Johnson, Steven. *Where Good Ideas Come From: The Natural History of Innovation*. New York: Riverhead Books, 2010.

Kahneman, Daniel. *Thinking, Fast and Slow*. New York: Farrar, Straus and Giroux, 2011.

Kelley, Tom, with Jonathan Littman. *The Art of Innovation: Lessons in Creativity from IDEO, America's Leading Design Firm*. New York: Doubleday, 2001.

Kotter, John P. *Leading Change*. Boston: Harvard Business School Press, 1996.

Minelli, Michael, Michele Chambers, and Ambiga Dhiraj. *Big Data, Big Analytics: Emerging Business Intelligence and Analytic Trends for Today's Businesses*. Hoboken, NJ: John Wiley & Sons, 2013.

Moore, Geoffrey A. *Dealing with Darwin: How Great Companies Innovate at Every Phase of Their Evolution*. New York: Portfolio/Penguin, 2005, 2008.

Prahalad, C. K., and M. S. Krishnan. *The New Age of Innovation: Driving Co-created Value Through Global Networks*. New York: McGraw-Hill, 2008.

Ridley, Matt. *The Rational Optimist: How Prosperity Evolves*. New York: HarperCollins, 2010.

Rosenstein, Bruce. *Living in More Than One World: How Peter Drucker's Wisdom Can Inspire and Transform Your Life*. San Francisco: Berrett-Koehler, 2009.

Senor, Dan, and Saul Singer. *Start-up Nation: The Story of Israel's Economic Miracle*. New York: Twelve/Hachette Book Group, 2011.

Tapscott, Don, and Anthony D. Williams. *Macrowikinomics: New Solutions for a Connected Planet*. New York: Portfolio/Penguin, 2010.

————. *Wikinomics: How Mass Collaboration Changes Everything*. New York: Portfolio/Penguin, 2008.

MEET OUR SOURCES

Rich Adduci is senior vice president and chief information officer at Boston Scientific. In his role as CIO, Rich has led the transformation of Boston Scientific's IS organization, creating a global IS organization focused on delivering competitive advantage for Boston Scientific through information and technology. Rich serves as a member of Boston Scientific's Operating Committee, Quality Management Board, and Capital Committee. Rich is actively engaged in shaping direction in the information technology community at large through his role on the Steering Committee for the SAP Life Sciences Advisory Committee, Model N Strategic Planning Team, and the Howard University School of Business MIS Program Advisory Board.

Prior to joining Boston Scientific, Rich was a partner at Accenture. During his 18-year career at Accenture, Rich was a leader in Accenture's Health and Life Science practice, leading the contracting excellence and supply chain practices within the health and life sciences industry vertical. Rich holds more than 15 European patents and two U.S. patents for the development of modeling tools to support business strategy and market entry for new wireless technologies.

Rich earned a bachelor of science in industrial engineering from Purdue University and an MBA from the University of Chicago with concentrations in finance and economics. He is an active member of his community and presently serves on the Boston-area American Heart Association Executive Board and is chairman of BSC's 2012 Boston AHA Heart Walk event.

* * *

F. Thaddeus Arroyo is chief information officer at AT&T Services, Inc. He was appointed to his current position in January 2007, following the close of the merger among AT&T, Bell-South, and Cingular. In his role, he is responsible for directing the company's internal IT organization and infrastructure, including Internet and intranet capabilities, developing applications systems across the mobility and home solutions markets, business and network solutions segments, and AT&T's corporate systems. He also oversees AT&T's enterprise data centers. As AT&T's CIO, Thaddeus has successfully advanced technology initiatives while rationalizing AT&T's enterprise application portfolio, driving service platform rationalization, and improving operational processes.

Prior to joining AT&T, Thaddeus served as CIO at Cingular Wireless and prior to that he served as senior vice president of product marketing and development for Sabre Corporation. His responsibilities included infrastructure development, deployment, strategic planning, and data network services. Prior to joining Sabre, Thaddeus was employed in Southwestern Bell's IT organization.

Under Thaddeus's leadership, AT&T was recognized by *Computerworld* as one of the 100 best companies to work for in IT for 2012 and by the American Business Awards as the 2009 IT Department of the Year for innovation and contribution to AT&T's business goals. In addition, AT&T has been an *InformationWeek* 500 award recipient for five consecutive years and a CIO 100 award recipient in five of the last six years, which honors those companies that are transforming business through innovation and execution.

Thaddeus has a bachelor's degree in mathematics from the University of Texas at Arlington, and an MBA from Southern Methodist University.

* * *

Saad Ayub is senior vice president and chief information officer for Scholastic Inc. He is a senior information services executive who has led IT organizations and provided technology consultation within the financial, telecom, media, education, publishing, and healthcare industries. He is a technology strategist who has driven various digital transformations and formulated new business models. As a business technology leader of large application and infrastructure teams, Saad has transformed organizations, developed new revenue opportunities leveraging emerging and digital technologies, decreased business costs through efficient use of technology, and streamlined IT platforms (applications and infrastructure) to improve costs and time to market.

As SVP and CIO at Scholastic, he is responsible for transforming the IT organization that enables Scholastic to capitalize on the current and future digitalization trends of the media and education industry. He is also accountable for partnering with the business to drive the evolution of the business model that enables growth through the use of digital technologies.

Saad has diverse experience ranging from applied research to management consulting. He has worked as a research scientist in the field of artificial intelligence at GE Corporate Research and Development and GTE Labs. He has worked as a management consultant with McKinsey & Company, where he worked with clients on technology strategy and transformation of IT organizations. Additionally, he worked as a divisional CIO at The Hartford and Aetna.

Saad has published numerous papers in the field of artificial intelligence. He has been a speaker on a number of IT leadership topics at various conferences. Saad is a recipient of the *Computerworld* Premier 100 IT Leaders Award. He has a BSc in computer engineering from METU in Ankara, Turkey, an MBA from Rensselaer Polytechnic Institute, and a PhD in computer science, also from Rensselaer.

* * *

Bruce Bachenheimer is a clinical professor of management, the director of the Entrepreneurship Lab, and a faculty fellow of the Wilson Center for Social Entrepreneurship at Pace University. He teaches undergraduate and graduate courses, primarily in the areas of entrepreneurship, management, and strategy. He is also the organizer of the annual Pace Pitch Contest and Business Plan competition.

He is a member of the board and past chair of the New York City chapter of the MIT Enterprise Forum and has served on the organization's global board. He serves on the board of directors and advisors of LeadAmerica and has served as a consultant to the New York City Department of Small Business Services, the New York City Economic Development Corporation, and a variety of new ventures. Bruce has been widely quoted in a variety of domestic and international publications, interviewed on radio and television, and spoken on entrepreneurship for numerous organizations, including the Youth Assembly at the United Nations, the Global Consortium of Entrepreneurship Centers, the Kairos Society, and the U.S. Department of State's International Visitor Leadership Program and Foreign Press Center.

His earlier career includes serving as a vice president of iQ Venture Partners, an assistant vice president of Westpac Banking Corp., and an international banking officer for the Bank of Tokyo. As the international product manager for MSI, an SBA-certified 8(a) firm, he was responsible for the initial commercialization of a high-technology forensic science system. In that position, he conducted business in over 20 countries. Bruce was also the founder of Annapolis Maritime Corp. and the cofounder of StockCentral Australia. Other activities include having sailed his 36-foot boat from New England through the Caribbean to South America and back.

Bruce holds a BBA, summa cum laude, from Pace University. He spent a semester at Tsukuba National University in Japan as an undergraduate and continued to study Japanese at NYU after graduating. He later received the McKinsey & Company Leadership Scholarship to pursue an MBA degree, which he earned from the Australian Graduate School of Management. You can visit his web page at http://webpage.pace.edu/bbachenheimer.

* * *

Ramón Baez is senior vice president and chief information officer of Hewlett-Packard, responsible for the global information technology strategy and all of the company's IT assets that support HP employees and help drive strategic company priorities. This includes worldwide application development and the company's private cloud, IT security, data management, technology infrastructure, and telecommunication networks.

Ramón's career spans more than three decades with global Fortune 100 companies in industries including manufacturing, packaged goods, aerospace and defense, and products and services for the scientific community.

Prior to HP, he was vice president of information technology services and CIO of Kimberly-Clark Corp., where he was responsible for leading the company's enterprise-wide information systems initiatives. Before Kimberly-Clark, he served in CIO roles for Thermo Fisher Scientific Inc. and Honeywell's Automation and Control Solution group. He began his career at Northrop Grumman, where he spent 25 years and finished as CIO for its electronics systems sensor sector.

Ramón graduated from the University of La Verne in California with a bachelor's degree in business administration.

*   *   *

N S Bala is the senior vice president for the Manufacturing and High-Tech Industry Strategic Business Unit of Wipro

Technologies. He manages the P&L for this division, which contributes over 20 percent of the global revenues of Wipro Technologies. The 8,000-strong division focuses on enabling organizations in the manufacturing industry transform their business in an ever-changing economic environment by using IT as a lever to make them more agile and responsive across the entire value chain (areas such as customer management, manufacturing, supply chain, and product engineering).

Over the years, he has restructured the business unit to deepen its focus on specific subindustry segments, building a strong customer advisory capability and offering integrated services across business process, applications, and infrastructure. He has also been instrumental in driving innovation in delivery through models such as the Factory Model and the Center for Integrated Global Management of Applications (Cigma).

During his stint at Wipro, N S went through the transformation experienced in the Indian IT industry and has also been a key contributor to Wipro's journey in becoming one of the prominent players among the global service providers.

N S has been instrumental in pioneering the use of Toyota Production Systems principles in application and software development that was developed into a case study by the Harvard Business School and is being taught at the institute to MBAs. He was invited by Harvard to speak on the case study. The delivery model has also been featured in the book *Bangalore Tiger* by Steve Hamm. His recent innovation, Cigma, won Wipro the NASSCOM Innovation Award.

N S holds an MBA from the Indian Institute of Management, Kolkata, one of the premier management institutes in India.

* * *

Linda Ban is the Global C-suite Study director for the IBM Institute for Business Value (IBV). Linda's background includes more than 25 years in IT, business and operations strategy, and systems development. Her career focus has been in anticipating the next "new thing" and bridging the technical and business sides of the organization—ensuring that technology solutions support the objectives of the enterprise as a whole. Linda has extensive experience in running large programs, ranging from enterprise system implementations and upgrades to organization-wide communication networks. In addition to these roles, she also has extensive experience in creating, implementing, and over-seeing the accompanying organizations that provide operational support for both the technical and business side of these functions.

In her current role as the Global C-suite Study director, she provides leadership, strategy, and program oversight for the overall IBM C-suite Study program within IBV, where IBM has interviewed more than 18,000 C-suite executives face-to-face during the last nine years. She works with global teams to focus on trend identification and strategies that address critical business challenges faced by companies globally. In addition to her leadership role for the overall program, she has published extensively on a broad range of business topics, challenges, and solutions.

* * *

Mike Barlow is an award-winning journalist, author, and editor. Since launching his own firm, Cumulus Partners, he has represented major organizations in numerous industries.

Mike is coauthor of *The Executive's Guide to Enterprise Social Media Strategy* (Wiley, 2011) and *Partnering with the CIO* (Wiley, 2007). He has written numerous articles and white papers on marketing strategy, marketing automation, customer intelligence, collaborative social networking, cloud computing, and big data analytics.

Over the course of his career, Mike was a reporter and editor at several respected suburban daily newspapers, including the *Journal News* and the *Stamford Advocate*. His feature stories and columns appeared regularly in the *Los Angeles Times*, *Chicago Tribune*, *Miami Herald*, *Newsday*, and other major U.S. dailies.

* * *

Puneet Bhasin is chief information officer and senior vice president, technology, logistics, and customer service, for Waste Management. He is responsible for the company's information technology, logistics, and customer service operations. Prior to joining Waste Management, he held roles as SVP, global product and technology, and CIO, North America, for Monster Worldwide. Prior to that, he was an SVP for Putnam Investments and chief information officer for Ryder TRS.

Puneet received his BS degree from National Institute of Technology, India, and his MS degree from the Ohio State University.

* * *

Kendra M. Bonner is an organization effectiveness director specializing in global organization effectiveness, talent leadership, and coaching. Her work as an internal consultant has focused on leadership development, organization design, process reengineering, executive feedback, global interventions, curriculum management, and group facilitation.

She has consulted all over the United States and in Canada, Mexico, Germany, Japan, and China. She is fluent in Spanish and has leveraged her language skills to consult only in Spanish as she worked in Mexico for more than two years.

Her clients have included chief executives, vice presidents, first-line managers, and leadership teams. In her spare time, Kendra enjoys traveling with her husband and participating in competitive bodybuilding.

Kendra received a BA in psychology from Oklahoma State University, an MS in business management from Texas A&M University, and an MS in organization development from Pepperdine University. Kendra has 12 years of experience in leadership development with major companies, including Texas Instruments, JCPenney, and Mohawk/Dal-Tile.

* * *

Whitney Bouck is the general manager of Box Enterprise, responsible for driving the growth strategy for Box in the enterprise market across sales, marketing, product, and services. Box has built a very successful business in the midmarket, SMB, and consumer sectors, and has hired her to accelerate growth in selling to large corporations. Prior to joining Box in April 2011, she gained more than 20 years of experience in enterprise software in a variety of leadership roles.

Her most recent position prior to Box was as chief marketing officer for the Information Intelligence Group, a division of EMC. In this role, she was responsible for the division's global marketing strategy, branding, thought leadership, product marketing, and lead generation for the division's products and solutions, including EMC Documentum, EMC Captiva, and EMC SourceOne. Other aspects of Whitney's leadership include social media and community marketing, competitive intelligence, field enablement, pricing, and marketing communications.

Whitney joined EMC via the acquisition of Documentum in 2003. In 2004, she was appointed vice president of strategic marketing for EMC Software Group, which included solutions for content management, backup, archiving, recovery, and resource management. In this role, she heavily influenced the changing reputation of EMC from a hardware storage company to an information management company.

During the eight years she spent at Documentum prior to the acquisition, she held a variety of technical and marketing management positions. From 2002 to 2004, she served as vice president and general manager of the electronic document management and Web content management businesses, where she managed a worldwide team of engineers, product managers, and product marketing managers responsible for nearly half of Documentum's license revenues. From 1999 to 2002 she was vice president of worldwide product marketing.

Prior to Documentum, Whitney had a long career in the relational database market that included various product marketing, engineering, and other technical positions at Sybase and Oracle.

Whitney was a recipient of the Silicon Valley Women of Influence award in 2009 and the Top 40 Under 40 award in 2003. She is a frequent keynote speaker at numerous industry trade shows and conferences.

She also served on the board of directors for AIIM International from 2006 to 2010, and is a member of the Forum for Women Entrepreneurs and Executives as well as Women in Technology International (WITI). She was an executive sponsor of the Women's Leadership Forum at EMC for two years, and was a participant of the 2010 Leadership in the Fast Lane at EMC. Whitney holds a BA in philosophy, politics, and economics from Claremont McKenna College.

* * *

Gregory E. Buoncontri is executive vice president and chief information officer for Pitney Bowes Inc. He is responsible for the global management of the company's IT Shared Services unit (known as TechCentral) that provides systems development and maintenance, computer and network operations, technical support services, project management, technology planning and assessments, and relationships with key technology suppliers and partners. Greg is a corporate officer and a member of the senior management committee. He also chairs the company's transformation steering committee, which oversees productivity and business process initiatives.

Greg held similar responsibilities for Novartis Pharmaceuticals Corporation (formerly Sandoz Pharmaceuticals), commencing in 1994 when he joined the pharmaceutical industry. Following the merger of Sandoz and Ciba-Geigy in December of 1996, he directed the integration of those companies' IT functions as the CIO for Novartis IT activities in the United States. Prior to this, he was CIO at both ABB and Combustion Engineering, where he led the deployment of state-of-the-art financial, manufacturing, engineering, and scientific systems.

Greg grew up in New York City. He holds a bachelor's degree in history from Fairfield University. He and his wife, Barbara, have three children and two grandchildren.

*   *   *

Photo Credit: Steve Maller

Tim Campos is currently the chief information officer at Facebook, the world's largest social network. Prior to joining the team at Facebook, he served as the CIO and vice president of IT at KLA-Tencor and worked at Internet start-up Portera Systems, where he was responsible for engineering and hosting architecture.

He is a business-oriented technical leader with an emphasis in enterprise systems and application hosting services. With over 18 years of industry experience in both software engineering and information technology, he has a unique understanding of the challenges in both developing and applying information technology.

Tim has an MBA from Columbia University and a degree in electrical engineering and computer science from the University of California at Berkeley. He is on the board of directors for the Fisher IT Center at the Haas School of Business at the University of California at Berkeley, as well as on the advisory board for several Silicon Valley start-ups.

*   *   *

Photo Credit: Craig Toron

Mike Capone combines a unique blend of client-facing operational experience and strong technical knowledge. He guides both product development and IT as corporate vice president of product development and chief information officer for ADP, a leading provider of human capital management services and one of the world's largest providers of business process outsourcing solutions.

Under his leadership as CVP and CIO, ADP has earned accolades for its technology leadership and innovations. For example, ADP was named to *Forbes* magazine's list of "The World's Most Innovative Companies" for 2012 and *Computerworld*'s list of the "100 Best Places to Work in IT" for 2012, and was among the top 100 companies on the *InformationWeek* 500 for 2012, an annual list of the top business technology innovators in the United States.

Mike is a 24-year veteran of ADP and has held positions in product development, information technology, and operations. Prior to becoming CVP and CIO, he served as senior vice president and general manager of ADP GlobalView, an award-winning multilingual, multicurrency human resources outsourcing solution. In this role, he led ADP's efforts to develop a global HR BPO business for large multinational corporations in partnership with SAP. In addition to his day-to-day responsibilities, he is a trustee for ADP's charitable foundation and serves on the boards of several nonprofit organizations.

Mike earned a BS degree in computer science from Dickinson College and an MBA in finance from Pace University.

*   *   *

Sameer Dholakia is group vice president and general manager of the Cloud Platforms Group at Citrix, driving the company's product strategy for cloud infrastructure and server virtualization. He joined the company in 2010, when Citrix acquired VMLogix, where he served as CEO. Sameer brings extensive enterprise software experience to Citrix, having held key leadership roles in sales, business development, and product management at companies such as Trilogy, Inc.

He received bachelor's and master's degrees from Stanford University and an MBA from Harvard Business School.

* * *

Tim Dilley is executive vice president, worldwide services, and chief customer officer at NetSuite. He has more than 25 years of experience in technology customer service and has held executive management positions in professional services and customer support. At NetSuite, he is responsible for driving customer success and manages global teams in consulting, training, customer support, and client management. Prior to NetSuite, he was senior vice president of global customer services at Informatica, an associate partner for worldwide utilities at Andersen Consulting (Accenture), and a cofounder of Axiom Management Consulting.

Tim holds a BS in business administration from California State University at Fresno.

* * *

John Engates joined Rackspace in August 2000, just a year after the company was founded, as vice president of operations, managing the data center operations and customer service teams. Two years later, when Rackspace decided to add new services for larger enterprise customers, John created and helped develop the Intensive Hosting business unit.

Most recently, John has played an active role in the evolution and evangelism of Rackspace's cloud computing strategy and cloud products. John meets frequently with customers to hear about their needs and concerns, and to discuss Rackspace's vision for the future of cloud computing. John currently serves as chief technology officer.

He is also an internationally recognized cloud computing expert and a sought-after speaker at technology conferences. He speaks on the future of cloud computing, enterprise cloud adoption, data center efficiency, green data center best practices, and more. He is a graduate of the University of Texas at San Antonio and holds a BBA in accounting.

* * *

Carol Fawcett is chief information officer for the Dell Software Group. She serves as a strategic business partner to senior management. She is responsible for aligning and leveraging technology, architecture planning, answering global business needs, and providing Dell Software with a strategic advantage internally and externally in the market. Under her leadership, the IS team provides critical feedback to the business, as well as to prospects and external customers on the extensive internal use of Dell Software products.

Before joining Quest in 2000, she held IT leadership roles at Western Digital, Coldwell Banker, and Pacific Mutual. In her roles, Carol provided leadership in transformational activities for both IT and business in all areas of the enterprise business. Business strategies were met using combinations of on-premise and public cloud solutions for financials, manufacturing, CRM, HR/payroll, marketing/Web, data warehousing, and sales force automation. She has provided guidance for delivering a successful company-wide certification for ISO900x, adherence to Sarbanes-Oxley requirements, and successful M&A integration programs. Carol holds a bachelor's degree in management information systems with a minor in computer science from San Diego–based National University.

* * *

Jay Ferro is chief information officer for the American Cancer Society (ACS), a nationwide, community-based voluntary health organization dedicated to eliminating cancer as a major health problem. Headquartered in Atlanta, Georgia, the American Cancer Society has 12 chartered divisions, more than 900 local offices nationwide, and a presence in more than 5,100 communities. Jay is responsible for the people, strategy, and operations of the Global Information Technology organization.

Prior to joining ACS in 2012, Jay served as senior vice president and CIO for AdCare Health Systems, a rapidly growing and recognized innovator in health-care facility management. Jay spent the previous seven years at AIG (American

International Group), most recently as vice president and CIO for Chartis Aerospace (formerly AIG Aviation), a leading global aerospace insurer.

At Chartis, Jay implemented numerous improvements that have delivered substantial value to the organization while managing significant organizational change in a turbulent market environment. In addition to his role as associate vice president of IT with AIG Personal Lines, Jay was selected as chief finance officer for operations and systems in 2006 and led multiple global IT Finance and Governance Standards initiatives that resulted in millions of dollars in savings for the organization.

Jay continues to be a thought leader in the IT arena and is a frequent guest speaker and panelist, both in Atlanta and nationwide. In recognition of his accomplishments, Jay was selected as Georgia CIO of the Year in 2011 and is currently serving as vice chair for the Georgia CIO Leadership Association.

His commitment and dedication to community involvement is evidenced by the time and energy he contributes. In 2007, he founded the nonprofit group, Priscilla's Promise, in honor of his late wife, which raises funds for cervical cancer education and research, and currently serves as its executive director. In 2011, he was elected to the board of directors for TechBridge, an Atlanta-based nonprofit organization that helps other nonprofits use technology to improve their capability to serve the community.

Jay earned both his bachelor's degree in political science and his MBA from the University of Georgia. He continues to be involved with his alma mater, both as a mentor for young alumni and as a member of the alumni board of directors for the Terry College of Business.

Jay lives in the metro Atlanta area with his three amazing sons: Trey, Connor, and Alex.

* * *

Thomas Fountain is the chief technology officer of Pneuron Corporation, an emerging provider of enterprise software for building distributed analytics and applications solutions. In this role, he provides leadership of product strategy and positioning in the enterprise market, and works closely with customers to develop innovative solutions to their most pressing and complex business needs.

He joined Pneuron in late 2012 as the company was accelerating its entry into the enterprise market, and brings over 20 years of experience in large multinational companies, industries, and roles. Tom combines over 10 years in senior CIO leadership roles with proven expertise at improving business through programs that integrate information technology, organizational development, and process improvement techniques.

He was most recently consulting to start-up and emerging companies, providing strategic product and technology guidance to help them succeed in the Enterprise IT market. Previously, he served as Global CIO at Bunge, Ltd., a $50 billion global agribusiness with operations in over 30 countries. There he led IT strategy and governance to maximize leverage across Bunge's global footprint. Prior to Bunge, he served as VP and CIO of Honeywell Specialty Materials, a $5.2 billion manufacturer of specialty chemicals and engineered materials. There he accomplished strategic transformation of IT to a business value creation–focused organization and introduced both process consulting and change management services to serve internal customers during complex business change programs. His first role at Honeywell was as VP and CIO for the Engines, Systems, and Services business unit of Honeywell Aerospace. In that role he led the upgrade of investment and execution governance and partnered with Engineering to reduce new product introduction cycle time.

Earlier in his career, he was the global CIO at GE Silicones and the manager, technology and services, at GE Appliances. Fountain has also had product management, intelligence officer, and engineering positions with Dell, the Central Intelligence Agency, HP, and Martin-Marietta.

Tom attended the Massachusetts Institute of Technology and received a BS in electrical engineering. He later attended

Duke University, where he received an MS degree in electrical engineering as well as an MBA from Duke's Fuqua School of Business.

*   *   *

Photo Credit: Melanie Acevedo

Michelle Garvey was recently named senior vice president and chief information officer for ANN INC., one of the leading specialty retailers for fashionable women's clothing, serving clients across the United States, Puerto Rico, and now Canada. The company meets the needs of modern women's busy lifestyles by providing a full range of career, casual, and occasion offerings in one location, with collections planned with versatile styles that coordinate not only from head to toe but also from season to season, so that its customers can build a full wardrobe suitable to their needs from its collections at both its Ann Taylor and LOFT divisions.

Michelle previously held CIO positions with Warnaco, Brooks Brothers, Memberworks, and Sportmart, with previous experience at retailers such as Crate and Barrel, the

Registry Stores, and Ames Department Stores, after starting her career in consulting with Arthur Andersen. She holds a BS in civil engineering and an MBA in finance from Cornell University.

* * *

Doug Harr is the chief information officer at Splunk. He is responsible for the strategic use of technology at the company. Doug and his team serve Splunk's IT needs using private and public cloud solutions, while managing Web functionality and global facilities. He oversees corporate analytics, an internal Splunk implementation to deliver Web analytics, application management, security forensics, and operational intelligence for the company at large.

He has been leading IT organizations for most of his career, at companies such as Ingres Corporation, Portal Software, and Hewlett-Packard. The rest of the time he has been in the IT consulting field, focused on delivering enterprise business applications to clients and technology companies like Symantec, VMware, and Activision.

Doug holds a BS in business from Cal Poly, San Luis Obispo. He is engaged in the CISE CIO consortium, lectures at several local universities, and is a faculty member for the CIO Executive Development Program at San Francisco State University.

* * *

Peter High founded Metis Strategy in 2001. He is an expert in business and IT strategy, and has been a trusted advisor to a wide array of business and tech executives ranging across Fortune 500 companies in various industries. Peter has developed several strategic methodologies that he and his firm have taught clients to use on their own in order to develop and update strategic plans, choose and manage the right portfolio of projects, and ensure that team performance is on the path to world-class levels.

In December 2009 his book *World Class IT: Why Businesses Succeed When IT Triumphs* was published. In that same year it was named one of the top three IT books of 2009 by *CIO Insight*, and the number one book to read to "be smarter than your boss," according to *Baseline* magazine, among other accolades. Upon publication in China in late 2010, it climbed into the top 50 business books sold in that market.

Since 2008, Peter has moderated a widely listened-to podcast entitled *The Forum on World Class IT*, which is available through iTunes on a biweekly basis. He is a regular contributor to *Forbes* and *CIO Insight*, and has also written for the *Wall Street Journal*, *CIO*, *CIO Digest*, and *InformationWeek*, among other publications.

He has been the keynote speaker at a wide array of executive conferences and universities in the United States, Canada, China, India, and Australia, and he has lectured at several universities, including Georgetown University's McDonough School of Business, the University of Washington (Seattle) Foster School of Business, the University of Maryland's Smith School of Business, Virginia Commonwealth University's School of Business, Purdue University, and the National Defense University.

Prior to founding Metis Strategy, he worked in the strategy division of Luminant Worldwide, a full-service consulting firm, as a member of the management team. He began his career in consulting with Integral, Inc., an innovation management firm founded by the former dean of Harvard Business School, Kim Clark.

Peter graduated from the University of Pennsylvania with degrees in economics and history.

* * *

Mike Hill is vice president of Enterprise Initiatives for IBM and is responsible for the development and delivery of new information technologies and services. With an initial focus on cloud computing, Mike is leading the IBM sales, services, and business development teams to provide a portfolio of cloud-delivered solutions for clients.

Prior to this position, Mike was general manager of IBM Global Telecommunications Industry, working with IBM clients to help them succeed in a converging ecosystem. By embracing open standards and end-to-end integration, Mike believes that telecommunications companies can increase their ability to sustain value and compete in a changing market.

His other positions have included vice president of business transformation and CIO responsible for IBM's global voice and data infrastructure and application development. Mike also was a member of the executive team that managed IBM's internal transformation to an e-business in the 1990s, an initiative that helped turn IBM's business into a new model of growth in the twenty-first century. Prior to this,

Mike held many sales and executive management positions, including general manager of IBM Southeast and South Asia.

Mike earned a B.S. in electrical engineering from the University of Florida and joined IBM in 1978.

*   *   *

Daphne E. Jones is senior vice president and chief information officer, Hospira, Inc., the world leader in specialty generic injectable pharmaceuticals and infusion technologies. In her role as SVP and CIO, Daphne is accountable for helping the $4 billion company to achieve and sustain market leadership through the use of technical solutions across multiple functions around the world. Reporting to the CEO and chairman of the board, she and her diverse team of IT professionals, who are located across the United States, Asia-Pacific, EMEA (Europe, Middle East, and Africa), and India, help define and ensure implementation of strategies and improved business processes designed to deliver increased market share, revenue, profitability, compliance, and overall business value. She is accountable for the worldwide solution strategy and value, business process performance improvement, and global technology portfolio.

Most recently, Daphne served as the worldwide vice president of information technology and chief information officer for Johnson & Johnson's Ortho-Clinical Diagnostics, Inc., where she steered the implementation of multiregional SAP solutions and collaborated with Integrated Hospital Networks in the area of health-care IT. As CIO, Daphne also developed and executed global IT strategies across multiple business units, and drove Johnson & Johnson's MD&D IT transformation.

She has recently been named as a *Computerworld* Premier 100 IT Leader for 2012, received the 2012 Executive Buyer Diversity Award from MBEIC, the BDPA "CIO Innovator Award," and was awarded the United Way of NYC Women in Philanthropy Award.

She is a member of the Economic Club of Chicago (membership committee), the IT Senior Management Forum (ITSMF), and the Executive Leadership Council, is a board of trustee for the Evanston Arts Center, and serves on the Executive Council of the National Biotechnology & Pharmaceutical Association. In 2009 and 2010, until Mayor Richard M. Daley left office, she served on his Council for Technology Advisors (and also chaired the HealthCare IT Subcommittee).

Daphne received a BS in business administration and an MBA from Illinois State University.

* * *

Hunter Jones is vice president, enterprise services, and chief information officer for Cameron International. Based in Houston, he reports to the chief executive officer of Cameron, a global oilfield services company with over 28,000 employees in more than 350 locations with major manufacturing facilities in 19 countries. The enterprise services element, consisting of HSSE, supply chain, technology and development, and continuous improvement activities, was recently added to Hunter's role as chief information officer, which he has held since October 2009. During his tenure as CIO he has seen Cameron grow by 10,000 employees, completed the consolidation of business unit information technology organizations into an enterprisewide unit, and led an ongoing enterprise-level business transformation process that includes a major ERP implementation.

Prior to his CIO position he held the position of vice president, surface operations, with responsibility for 11 manufacturing facilities around the world, including building new facilities in Romania and China. Leading to that role he held leadership positions in the manufacturing, supply chain, and quality organizations within Cameron.

This background allowed him the opportunity to travel the world extensively and understand the people and processes that were required to make Cameron successful.

Before joining Cameron in 1996 he worked 15 years for GE, starting his career on their Manufacturing Management program. After completing that program he moved through a progression of manufacturing and supply chain positions and locations in the aerospace and power systems businesses, including a plant management position for the aerospace manufacturing facility in King of Prussia, Pennsylvania.

Hunter graduated from the University of Florida with a degree in industrial engineering and serves on the advisory board of the department.

* * *

Sheila B. Jordan is senior vice president of communication and collaboration IT at Cisco Systems, reporting to CIO Rebecca Jacoby. She is responsible for delivering and integrating key IT services that touch Cisco's global workforce. Her goal is to drive productivity and a superior, holistic end-user experience for all employees through an integrated architectural approach. She oversees a worldwide team of more than 500 IT professionals. Within her purview are the following areas: collaboration platforms; communications, collaboration, and mobility services; user experience; and support for C-level Cisco executives.

Sheila joined Cisco in 2005 from Walt Disney World in Orlando, Florida, where she was SVP of Destination Disney.

She holds a BA in accounting from the University of Central Florida and an MBA from Florida Institute of Technology.

* * *

Mike Kail is vice president of IT operations at Netflix, leading a team of 90 employees in his organization. He is an experienced professional with over 20 years of IT operations executive leadership experience who focuses on highly scalable architecture.

Before joining Netflix, he was the VP of IT operations at Attensity, where he was responsible for various big data components as well as the integration of Americas and the EMEA (Europe, Middle East, and Africa) IT teams. He specializes in Unix system/network architecture, SaaS/cloud deployments, Hadoop/HBase clusters, monitoring/alerting, SQL/NoSQL, virtualization, and performance tuning/scalability.

Mike has a bachelor's degree in computer science from Iowa State University.

*   *   *

Jim Knight is global chief information officer and executive vice president at Chubb and Son Insurance Company. As global CIO, he provides vision and leadership to maximize the usage of information technology to create and maintain leadership for the Chubb Corporation worldwide. Jim is a Project Management Professional (PMP) and he serves on the boards of the Society of Information Management–International (executive vice chair) and the Association for Cooperative Operations Research and Development (ACORD).

He brings over 30 years of experience in the delivery and management of information technology, primarily in the property and casualty insurance industry. Prior to Chubb, Jim worked at Utica National Insurance Company, Home Insurance Company, and Merck-Medco.

Jim holds a BA in computer science from Utica College and a master of MIS from Kennedy-Western University.

* * *

Dr. William R. LaFontaine Jr. is vice president, technical strategy and worldwide operations, research, at IBM. He is responsible for setting the direction of IBM's overall research strategy across 11 worldwide labs and leading the global operations and information systems teams. In this capacity, he leads the annual creation of the Global Technology Outlook,

3- to 10-year technology projections that influence IBM's R&D directions along with acquisition strategies.

He previously held the position of general manager, global technology services, Middle East and Africa. In this role, he had the mandate to drive hyper growth for IBM services business in this emerging market, including opening new countries in Africa for IBM. During his tenure in Africa, IBM expanded its services operations in more than 13 countries. Prior to this role, Bill was vice president, licensing and business development, for IBM's intellectual property business. In this capacity, he had the worldwide responsibility for licensing IBM's patent, trademark, and domain name portfolio. In addition, his team played a critical role in the creation of technology-based strategic alliances with partners around the world. In previous positions at IBM, Bill was vice president, corporate strategy, and vice president, worldwide sales and service, for IBM Technology Group.

During his 20-plus-year career at IBM he led product and process development teams as well as sales, marketing, and operations organizations in Japan, Singapore, and North America. Bill's international experience includes assignments in Japan, Singapore, and South Africa. He is the recipient of several U.S. and native patents.

Bill holds a bachelor's degree in metallurgical engineering from Cal Poly, San Luis Obispo, and received his MS and PhD degrees in materials science and engineering from Cornell University.

*   *   *

Jonathan Landon is the director of IT strategy, technology, and architecture, Kimberly-Clark. He is responsible for the development and implementation of global strategy, business planning, overall technological direction, architecture, and governance for the IT services function. A key aspect of this role is to assure that Kimberly-Clark's IT investments fully integrate with and measurably contribute to the realization of the corporation's global business plan.

He joined Kimberly-Clark in 1980 in Toronto. Since then he has held numerous positions of increasing responsibility in virtually all aspects of the IT field. He has held country, regional, and global leadership positions in the United States, Asia-Pacific, Europe, the Middle East and Africa, and Canada. Jonathan assumed his current position in November 2008.

Jonathan has a BA in business management and communication from Concordia University Wisconsin.

* * *

Françoise LeGoues is the vice president for Innovation Initiatives in IBM's CIO's organization. She and her team are responsible for identifying, testing, and transferring emerging technologies that have the potential for transforming IBM and the way IBMers work, communicate, and innovate.

She joined the IBM Research Division after getting a PhD in material sciences from Carnegie-Mellon University. As a research staff member, and then as the manager of the "Materials Characterization" group, she authored over 150 scientific publications and obtained 4 patents.

She then held a number of positions at IBM, all of which had the common thread of bringing innovation to clients and to IBMers. As the manager of the Industry Solutions Lab, she managed three Solutions Labs worldwide, where customers can see, touch, and play with the new technologies that IBM scientists are inventing, and where they can also discuss and mold the use of these technologies in their own businesses.

She also ran the First-of-a-Kind program, which seeds the deployment of emerging technologies to create innovation in the marketplace through joint research and customer engagements.

As the director of innovation in the Applications Management Services business unit, she built a team of senior IT architects to help grow the AMS business through technical leadership.

In her most recent role as vice president and chief technology officer for the Distribution Sector, in IBM's Sales and Distribution organization, she uses innovation throughout IBM to help define and build new industry solutions and to help clients define their own technology strategy.

She is an IBM Distinguished Engineer and a member of the IBM Academy.

* * *

Tony Leng is a managing director of Diversified Search and leads the CIO and technology practices. Previously, he was managing partner of Hodge Partners and headed up the CIO and technology practices for this retained executive search firm. His clients include public and private companies, where he has placed CIOs and other senior-level IT executives, including organizations such as Delta Dental, Kaiser Permanente, Blue Shield of California, Esurance, Dignity Heath, Visa, Franklin Templeton, Wells Fargo, and Levi Strauss.

Tony has built a thriving technology practice comprised of candidates and clients who seek out his services time and again. He uses his operating experience, combined with the knowledge that he has gained in the search industry, to drill down and understand at a nuanced level what his clients are seeking to achieve as they build their IT teams. His experience in working at both large and small companies has made him particularly effective in understanding the challenges and leadership requirements that businesses face.

He has developed a deep and broad network. He is frequently asked to speak on panels to address key topics and emerging issues affecting and driving today's technology. He has facilitated a monthly CIO forum for the past eight years. The forum was established as a venue for CIOs to discuss topics of relevance in their daily lives, and has afforded CIOs the opportunity to develop a close network to talk about current challenges in a peer group environment on a confidential basis. Participating companies have included Gap, Levi Strauss, McKesson, Clorox, Matson, Kaiser Permanente, Williams-Sonoma, Bebe, Raley's, Restoration Hardware, Visa,

Cost Plus, Ross Stores, VMware, Facebook, Charles Schwab, Delta Dental, Macys.com, Fusion Storm, Facebook, BioRad, Salesforce.com, Safeway, Franklin Templeton, BMC Software, and Blue Shield, among others.

Tony received a bachelor of commerce (with honors) from the University of Cape Town, South Africa. He is qualified as a chartered accountant and CPA.

*   *   *

Ralph Loura is chief information officer for the Clorox Company, where he is responsible for the company's worldwide use of information technology. In his role, Ralph leads the global IT organization and directs the company's strategic technology initiatives in support of Clorox's goal of making everyday life better, every day.

Prior to joining Clorox, he served as SVP and CIO for Medicis, VP and CIO for Symbol Technologies, and held IT leadership positions at Cisco Systems, Lucent Technologies, and AT&T.

Ralph received a bachelor's degree in computer science–mathematics from Saint Joseph's College and a master's degree in computer science from Northwestern University.

* * *

Brian R. Lurie was recently appointed vice president and chief information officer for Gardner Denver Incorporated, a global manufacturer of industrial compressors, blowers, pumps, loading arms, and fuel systems. The company has 40 manufacturing facilities located in the Americas, EMEA (Europe, Middle East, and Africa), and Asia-Pacific, with offices in 33 different countries producing revenues of almost $2.5 billion annually.

Previously he served as the senior vice president and chief information officer of Teleflex Incorporated, a $2.4 billion critical care medical device manufacturer. For the prior 13 years he was the vice president and chief information officer at Stryker Orthopaedics, the largest operating division of the Stryker Corporation, with more than $7 billion in annual sales. Brian provides worldwide IT leadership and is presently responsible for all computer and communications requirements and has a core focus on customer satisfaction and response. In addition, he has more than 28 years of experience in the field of information technology. He has received many accolades, including the CIO Leadership Networks 2008 Top 10 Leaders & Innovators Award and 2009 *Computerworld* Premier 100 IT Leaders Award. He is a charter board member on the Temple University Computer and Information Sciences Advisory Board. He is also a technology guest speaker at the University of Pennsylvania and Columbia University.

Brian received a BA in computer and information sciences from Temple University and conducted postgraduate work at the University of Pennsylvania, Harvard University, and Gallup's Leadership Academy.

* * *

Arthur C. McAdams III is a versatile and dynamic executive and educator. He is director of graduate studies and senior lecturer at the University of Bridgeport, an adjunct professor at Fairfield University, and an independent management consultant.

A former chief information officer at SSC Inc., senior vice president at People's Bank, and lead programmer at Pitney Bowes, he led several successful strategic initiatives during his 30 years in industry. His areas of expertise are leadership, management, organization, strategy, quality, knowledge management, and information systems. His research has been published in the *International Journal of Technology, Knowledge & Society*, and the *Information Management Journal*.

Art holds a BS in general studies from Fairfield University, an MBA from the University of Connecticut, and a PhD in information systems from Nova Southeastern University.

* * *

Chris McGugan is vice president and general manager of Emerging Products and Technology at Avaya. The role includes responsibility for software development, product management, and marketing. Emerging Products and Technology includes DevConnect, Avaya's third-party developer network, cloud solutions, contact center, and UC applications as well as research into various forms of collaboration technologies.

Most recently, Chris was Avaya's vice president of product management for contact center solutions from 2008 to 2011. The role included responsibility for product roadmaps, architecture, and overall direction of the contact center offers.

Prior to this, Chris was vice president of products and engineering at Belkin, a leader in the consumer electronics market, where he led the overall product portfolio, design, and research and development efforts for their consumer and commercial product lines.

He is active in many technology standards bodies and industry associations, helping to drive the advancement of networking technology.

Chris is an alumnus of North Carolina State University.

* * *

Todd McKinnon is the chief executive officer and cofounder of Okta, the first cloud-based identity management platform.

Founded in 2009, Okta helps companies of all sizes secure their users, applications, and data—both in the cloud and behind the firewall—so work gets done, from any device, anywhere. Under Todd's leadership, Okta has grown into the leading identity solution, with hundreds of enterprise customers.

From 2003 to 2009, Todd was overall head of engineering at Salesforce.com, where he helped grow the team from 15 people to more than 250, and the service from two million daily transactions to more than 150 million with industry-leading performance and reliability. Todd's team developed and launched Force.com, the industry's first platform-as-a-service product, and AppExchange, the first online marketplace for cloud computing applications. Prior to joining Salesforce .com, Todd spent nearly a decade working in various engineering and leadership roles at PeopleSoft.

Todd currently serves on the board of directors for Family House, a not-for-profit organization that provides temporary housing to families of seriously ill children receiving treatment at the University of California–San Francisco Children's Hospital. Todd is a regular contributor to industry publications, including *Forbes*, *Fast Company*, and *Fortune*.

Todd earned a BS in business from Brigham Young Univeristy and an MS in computer science from Cal Poly, San Luis Obispo.

* * *

Photo Credit: M. Roselli

Michael Minelli is a sales and marketing expert with over 16 years of experience in the business analytics solutions space. Currently, he is vice president of sales and global alliances, information services, for MasterCard Advisors, where he is responsible for leading sales and strategic alliances that monetize MasterCard's data assets. MasterCard data assets encompass 1.8 billion cards, representing 34 million merchants in 210 countries and territories.

Prior to joining MasterCard Advisors, Mike led Revolution Analytics' sales team. He was responsible for both new business development and strategic alliances for the firm's software and services offerings supporting the Open Source R project.

Michael built his foundation and expertise in analytic solution sales and marketing as a sales director and global account manager at SAS. During his 11 years in multiple roles at SAS, he established an extremely successful track record in sales of large-scale analytic projects associated with customer intelligence, risk management, supply chain, and finance.

He is the coauthor of two successful business books, *Big Data, Big Analytics* (Wiley, 2013), and *Partnering with the CIO: The Future of IT Sales Seen Through the Eyes of Key Decision Makers* (Wiley, 2007).

Michael holds a BA in marketing from Pace University.

*   *   *

Gordon Payne leads the Citrix Desktop and Cloud division, overseeing the company's strategy for its virtualization, networking, and cloud products. These Citrix products make it easy for people to work and play from anywhere, providing IT a more efficient, secure, and cost-effective way to deliver applications and data to the people in their organization.

He engages with a wide range of customers, partners, and the talented Citrix product teams building a new model for IT-as-a-service. In this new model, organizations of all sizes can deliver IT services from both private and public clouds.

The people leveraging these services have the choice of working securely on any device from anywhere.

He has held a number of product division roles at Citrix, before taking on the Desktop and Cloud division in August 2011. He joined Citrix in 2004 with the acquisition of Net6. Prior to this, he held executive and general management roles in both start-ups and in larger corporations such as Nortel, where he spent more than a decade focused on private and public networking. He has lived and worked in Canada, the United Kingdom, Switzerland, Australia, and the United States, now working from the Citrix development center in the heart of Silicon Valley.

Gordon holds a bachelor's degree in commercial studies from the University of Western Ontario in Canada and an MBA from IMD in Lausanne, Switzerland.

* * *

Don Peppers is a bestselling business author and founding partner of Peppers & Rogers Group, the world's foremost customer-centered management consulting firm. Don is recognized as a global authority on marketing and business competition, and is widely credited with having launched the CRM revolution in the 1990s. A genuine thought leader, he was listed by the *Times* of London as one of the "Top 50 Business Brains." Accenture named him one of the "Top 100 Business Intellectuals," and the UK's Chartered Institute for Marketing called him one of the 50 "most influential thinkers in marketing and business today."

Don has a popular voice in the worldwide media, writing articles, sharing his point of view, and appearing frequently as an "expert blogger" for Fastcompany .com. He has authored or coauthored a legacy of international business bestsellers that have collectively sold over a million copies in 18 languages: *Extreme Trust: Honesty as a Competitive Advantage* (2012), *Managing Customer Relationships* (2011), *Rules to Break and Laws to Follow* (2008), *Return on Customer* (2005), *One to One B2B* (2001), *The One to One Manager* (1999), *The One to One Fieldbook* (1999), *Enterprise One to One* (1997), *Life's a Pitch: Then You Buy* (1995), and *The One to One Future* (1993).

*　*　*

Steve Phillips is senior vice president and chief information officer for Avnet, Inc., reporting to Avnet CEO Rick Hamada. He is also a member of the Avnet Executive Board and a corporate officer.

He came to Avnet with the 2005 acquisition of Memec, where he had served as SVP and CIO since 2004. Prior to joining Memec, he was SVP and CIO for Gateway Inc. He joined Gateway in 1999 and served as vice president of information technology in London and San Diego before his appointment in 2003 to CIO.

Steve is chairman of the board of Wick Communications, a private newspaper and specialty publication company. He is also chairman emeritus on the board of the Arizona Technology Council, a trade association that connects, represents, and supports Arizona's technology industry. He served as chairman from 2008 through 2011.

Under Steve's IT leadership, Avnet has been recognized with multiple awards, including the *CIO* 100, *Computerworld* Top Green-IT Vendor Organizations, and *InformationWeek* 500. Additionally, *Computerworld* named him a Premier 100 IT Leader in 2011. This lifetime recognition honors executives for exceptional technology leadership, innovative ideas to address business challenges, and effectively managing IT strategies.

Steve holds a BSc (Hons) in electronic engineering from Essex University and a postgraduate diploma in management studies from Thames Valley University. He is a fellow of the Institution of Engineering and Technology.

*   *   *

Brian Queenin is a partner in IBM's Business Analytics and Optimization practice with responsibility for the Midwest, Great West, and Pacific markets. Brian has significant experience

improving business and operational performance by implementing technology-based solutions for a broad range of companies
in many industries. Information technology solutions have en-
compassed design and development of business intelligence and
analytical engagements, performance management solutions,
decision support systems, sales force automation, trade promo-
tion, and analytical engagements. He has developed market-
ready products that have contributed to his clients' understanding and future vision for their business intelligence initiatives.
These offerings have provided a solid starting point for clients BI
and EPM engagements. He has experience in leading and directing consulting practices in North America and globally, serving
large clients and complex initiatives. Brian has been a requested
speaker at meetings, conferences, and seminars and sought after
by the analysts for his insights into the BI and EPM marketplace.
He is on the advisory board of several companies, assisting them
with market strategy and general management insight.

*   *   *

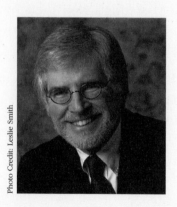

Photo Credit: Leslie Smith

Bruce Rosenstein is managing editor of *Leader to Leader*,
a publication of the Frances Hesselbein Leadership Institute

(formerly the Leader to Leader Institute and earlier the Peter F. Drucker Foundation for Nonprofit Management), and Jossey-Bass.

He is the author of *Living in More Than One World: How Peter Drucker's Wisdom Can Inspire and Transform Your Life* (2009). He worked for *USA Today* newspaper for 21 years, until late 2008, as a researcher in the news section and during the final 12 years also as a writer about business and management books for the money section.

Since 1996, he has taught as a lecturer at the Catholic University of America's School of Library and Information Science in Washington, DC. The Special Libraries Association/SLA announced in June 2012 that he was one of two recipients of the 2012 Rose L. Vormelker Award for "dedication to mentoring, outstanding instruction in graduate school settings, and their own professional achievements."

Bruce has a BA from the American University and an MSLS from the Catholic University of America's School of Library and Information Science. His website is www .brucerosenstein.com.

* * *

William Ruh is vice president of GE's Software and Analytics Center. He is responsible for setting and leading the software services and solutions portfolio strategy, development, and operations across all of GE. His team develops software to power the industrial Internet, a living network of intelligent machines and systems designed to advance industry and improve lives. These systems and solutions put data to work for GE's customers, giving businesses intelligent insight to make more sustainable and safe products.

Bill has more than 25 years of industry experience in enterprise application integration and object-oriented technology. Previously he was vice president at Cisco, where he held global responsibility for developing advanced services and solutions. Before that, he served as executive vice president and chief technology officer of Concept Five Technologies, Inc. Prior to that, he served as the chief technology officer and senior vice president of Software AG, Inc., where he was responsible for the growth and expansion of the solutions and consulting services team to provide customers with customized and industry-specific solutions.

Bill earned a BS and MS in computer science from California State University, Fullerton.

*   *   *

Doug Schneider is vice president and chief technology officer for the Canadian division of Manulife Financial, a leading Canada-based financial services group with principal operations in Asia, Canada, and the United States. As CTO, Doug is accountable for the alignment of the division's technology vision with the company's business strategy, working collaboratively with the diverse businesses within Manulife in missions ranging from enterprise architecture and shared technical services to risk management. His team's goal is to integrate processes with technologies that deliver flexibility, agility, high quality, and measurable shareholder value.

As modern organizations increasingly turn to technology to help them understand, manage, and adapt to change, Doug sees how the role of IT has become fundamental to business strategy. Through leadership and innovation, the CTO team helps the business set and achieve its goals by effectively leveraging technology to understand what customers want, to get products and services to market more quickly, and to stay ahead of the competition.

Prior to joining Manulife in 2011, Doug held many executive positions in top Canadian companies within the fields of financial services, telecommunications, consulting, sales, and outsourcing.

Doug holds a bachelor of mathematics from the University of Waterloo.

* * *

Tony Scott joined Microsoft Corp. in February 2008 as corporate vice president and chief information officer.

Under his leadership, Microsoft IT is responsible for security, infrastructure, messaging, and business applications for all of Microsoft, including support of the product groups, the corporate business groups, and the global sales and marketing organization. He champions IT as a value-added business for Microsoft and works with all the company's groups to identify opportunities, structure IT solutions, and deliver measurable returns to the business. He is also the executive sponsor for Microsoft's operational enterprise risk management efforts and supports the integration of management principles from the Quality & Business Excellence team, which drives continuous and breakthrough process improvements across the company.

Tony helps ensure that Microsoft is the "first and best customer" of its own products. In addition to maintaining a globally integrated set of enterprise IT platforms built on Microsoft technology, his team deploys prerelease versions of Microsoft products throughout the company. The direction and feedback his team provides to Microsoft developers help them enhance products before their commercial release. His "first and best customer" initiatives help identify and capture new market opportunities while codeveloping innovations to software plus services. Tony and his teams also share their IT expertise with customers (via IT Showcase), providing them with firsthand insights on product deployments and the value of Microsoft technologies and services.

Before joining Microsoft, he was the senior vice president and chief information officer for the Walt Disney Company, where he led planning, implementation, and operations of Disney IT systems and infrastructure across the company. He also held the position of chief technology officer, information systems and services, at General Motors Corp., where he was responsible for defining the information technology computing and telecommunications strategy, architecture, and standards across all of GM's businesses globally. As vice president of information services at Bristol-Myers Squibb Co., he led the transformation of its technology infrastructure organization to a shared services model and the development of a corporate infrastructure to support implementation of SAP- and Web-based technologies. Scott's professional experience has also included assignments at Marriott International Inc., Cadren Systems, Sun Microsystems Inc., and PricewaterhouseCoopers.

Tony has a BS in information systems management from the University of San Francisco and also holds a juris doctorate with a concentration in intellectual property and international law from Santa Clara University.

* * *

Frank Slootman has served as ServiceNow's president and chief executive officer, and as a director, since May 2011.

Prior to joining ServiceNow, he was a venture partner with Greylock Partners, a venture capital firm, from January 2011 to April 2011, and served as an advisor to EMC Corporation from January 2011 to February 2012.

From July 2009 to January 2011, he served as president of the Backup Recovery Systems Division at EMC. From July 2003 to July 2009, Frank was president and chief executive officer of Data Domain, Inc., an electronic storage solution company, which was acquired by EMC in 2009. As the CEO of Data Domain, he blazed new trails creating a high-growth enterprise storage company that went public on NASDAQ in 2007.

Prior to joining Data Domain, he served as an executive at Borland Software Corporation from June 2000 to June 2003, most recently as senior vice president of Products. From March 1993 to June 2000, he held management positions for two enterprise software divisions of Compuware Corporation.

Frank holds undergraduate and graduate degrees in economics from the Netherlands School of Economics, Erasmus University Rotterdam.

*   *   *

David Smith is recognized as a leading strategic futurist who combines a 35-year IT and business career with strategic visioning to help organizations better prepare for the future. His career has spanned European and U.S. corporations, and he has worked in commercial and financial markets. He recognizes the importance of embracing new business models and technologies as they present themselves and understands the challenges that these present to large corporations in particular.

Before establishing Global Futures and Foresight, an independent futures research firm, he created and ran the Unisys Global Future Forum. Prior to that he was head of strategic marketing for their $2 billion global financial services business. He is an international keynote speaker and author of many works on embracing change and the drivers of change. He has advised the UK and European Union governments on strategic investment decisions and recently addressed the European Parliament on the strategic direction they should pursue in leveraging social media for economic and jobs growth.

David began his IT career in 1974 using mainframe technology and has seen each new technological wave impact what we do and how we do it, in both our personal and professional lives. He has observed that when a new technology takes hold we first do things differently, and then when we truly understand its transformational nature, we do different things—we change the process. David has undertaken computer operations, programming, systems analysis, and project management roles in international IT vendor and user firms. He developed specialized line-of-business software and has led global business development and implementation services teams. Much of this experience was put to use in strategic marketing roles at Unisys Corporation.

Today he leads a strategic marketing firm with analysts, researchers, and coaches who help organizations understand their propensity to change and define strategies to confront the future with renewed assurance. They take pride in helping organizations reduce risk and embrace innovation more purposefully.

* * *

Dave Smoley is chief information officer at AstraZeneca, a global biopharmaceutical company. Before joining Astra-Zeneca, he was senior vice president and chief information officer at Flextronics, a $30 billion, industry-leading, Fortune Global 500 electronics manufacturing services provider with more than 200,000 employees and operations in 30 countries. Leading IT publication *InformationWeek* recently ranked him as one of the top 50 Global CIOs—IT Leaders Changing the Business World.

Prior to working at Flextronics, he served as vice president and CIO of Honeywell's Aerospace Electronics Systems. His extensive IT career also includes management positions with General Electric, where he held the position of director and chief information officer for GE Power Controls in Barcelona, Spain.

Dave holds a bachelor's degree in computer science from Clemson University and a MBA from the University of Virginia.

* * *

Randall N. Spratt is executive vice president, chief information officer, and chief technology officer for McKesson Corporation. As CTO, he guides the overall technology direction for the company's health-care technology products, and provides support and guidance for application development processes company-wide. As CIO, he is responsible for all technology initiatives within the corporation.

Randy has been with McKesson for more than 18 years, most recently as chief process officer for McKesson Provider Technologies (MPT), the company's medical software and services division, based in Alpharetta, Georgia. He also managed MPT's Business Development, Information Technology, and Strategic Planning offices, as well as MPT's Technology Services business.

Prior to joining McKesson, he held executive positions of increasing responsibility at the start-up Advanced Laboratory Systems (ALS), culminating with the role of chief operations officer. ALS was acquired by HBOC in 1996, which in turn was acquired by McKesson in 1999, and Randy took on responsibility for HBOC's laboratory systems business shortly thereafter. Following the acquisition of HBOC by McKesson in 1999, he relocated to Georgia to become part of the reconstructed management team.

Randy earned a BS in biology, with a minor in computer science, from the University of Utah.

* * *

Tim Stanley is an independent consultant and former senior vice president of Enterprise Strategy + Cloud Innovation at Salesforce.com. He is also actively involved in several public and private company board of directors and advisory roles, and as an angel and venture capital investor in a variety of innovative companies.

Tim is a professor at the Merage School of Business at the University of California, Irvine (UCI). Prior to joining Salesforce, Tim was the president of Tekexecs, an executive advisory service and consultancy, and chief experience officer of Innovatects, a business innovation and technology incubator.

Previously, Tim was the chief innovation officer, chief information officer/chief technology officer, and the senior vice president of Innovation, Gaming, and Technology for Caesars/Harrah's Entertainment, responsible for many of the award-winning innovations and initiatives that enabled the company to grow into the largest casino, hospitality, and entertainment company in the world.

Before joining Harrah's, Tim was a partner with consulting firms USWeb and marchFIRST, where he developed and led the Travel and Entertainment practice for the firms, working with several leading airline, hospitality, travel, and gaming clients around the world. Prior to that role, he was the start-up CIO for JetBlue Airways and National Airlines, where he launched the companies on innovative platforms of Internet/cloud-based IT applications, infrastructure, and operations. He has also held various leadership positions in the United States and overseas in the areas of marketing, operations, IT, R&D, and consulting with Intel Corporation, Optima/KPMG, and Kimberly-Clark Corporation.

Tim was named *InformationWeek*'s "Chief of the Year" for his unique innovation, business, and IT roles and achievements. He has also been recognized as one of *InfoWorld*'s "Top 25 CTOs," *Interactive Week*'s "Top 25 Unsung Heroes of the Internet," and has received *CIO*'s 100 Innovators Award and *CIO Insight*'s Partners in Alignment award for his successful linkage of business strategy and technology. Tim has also led Harrah's to achieve the *CIO* 100 award; *Computerworld*'s "Best Places to Work in IT" for nine consecutive years; and the American Business Awards' "Best MIS & IT Organization."

Tim holds a BS in engineering from the University of Washington and a joint MBA in international business and technology management from Thunderbird School of Global Management and Arizona State University.

* * *

Kimberly Stevenson is vice president and chief information officer of Intel Corporation. She is responsible for the corporate-wide use of information technology. Intel's IT organization delivers leading technology solutions and services that enable Intel's business strategies for growth and efficiency. The IT organization is comprised of over 6,000 IT professionals worldwide.

Previously, she was vice president and general manager of Intel's Global IT Operations and Services. In this role she led both the strategic and tactical support of Intel's worldwide infrastructure components, including data centers, network and telecommunications, enterprise application support, client computing, and a 24/7 internal service desk.

Prior to joining Intel, Kimberly spent seven years at EDS, now HP Enterprise Services, holding a variety of positions including vice president of Worldwide Communications, Media, and Entertainment (CM&E) Industry Practice, and vice president of enterprise service management, where she oversaw the global development and delivery of enterprise services. Before joining EDS, she spent 18 years at IBM, holding several executive positions, including vice president of marketing and operations of the eServer iSeries division.

Kimberly has a bachelor's degree from Northeastern University and an MBA from Cornell University, where she is an appointed member of the Cornell University Johnson School Advisory Board.

*   *   *

Don Tapscott is one of the world's leading authorities on innovation, media, and the economic and social impact of technology. He is chief executive officer of the Tapscott Group, and was founder and chairman of the international think tank New Paradigm before its acquisition by Moxie Software. He is vice chair of Spencer Trask Collaborative Innovations, a new company building a portfolio of companies in the collaboration and social media space, and the inaugural fellow at the Martin Prosperity Institute.

Don has given more than 400 keynote speeches and presentations over the past five years, including opening TED Global in Edinburgh in 2012. His clients include top executives of many of the world's largest corporations and government leaders from many countries. In 2011 Don was renamed one of the 50 most influential living management thinkers in the world by Thinkers50, earning the ninth spot on the list. Over the last two decades Don has appeared on many such lists.

Don has authored or coauthored 14 widely read books about information technology in business and society. His most recent book, *Macrowikinomics: New Solutions for a Connected Planet* (Revised Paperback, 2012), coauthored by Anthony D. Williams, was originally released in September 2010 to tremendous acclaim from business executives and the media and was a runner-up for the Best Business Book of the Last Two Years. *Macrowikinomics* is the follow-up to *Wikinomics: How Mass Collaboration Changes Everything* (2006), also coauthored by Anthony D. Williams. *Wikinomics* was an international bestseller, number one on the 2007 management book charts and on the *New York Times* and *Bloomberg Businessweek* bestseller lists. Translated into 20 languages, *Wikinomics* was a finalist for the prestigious Financial Times/Goldman

Sachs Best Business Book award and was chosen as one of the best books of the year by a number of publications, including the *Economist*.

Don is a frequent writer for the *Huffington Post*, the *Wall Street Journal*, the *New York Times*, *Forbes*, *Business 2.0*, the *Financial Times*, *USA Today*, the *Guardian*, and *Bloomberg Businessweek*, and has been interviewed and quoted widely in the broadcast media, including CNN, CNBC, NBC, CBS, NPR, Fox News, and the BBC.

He is involved extensively in the transformation of education, working with universities, school boards, and educational secretaries and ministers around the world. He also works with government leaders around the world to reinvent government for the digital era and strengthen democratic institutions. He is a member of the World Economic Forum, having served on several of the forum's Global Agenda Councils, and has attended Davos for a dozen years. Don is currently chair of the Forum's Working Group on New Platforms for Global Cooperation, Governance, and Problem Solving and is leading the definitive investigation into multi-stakeholder networks in collaboration with the Martin Prosperity Institute.

Deeply committed to the issue of mental health, he is a former member of the board of trustees of the Clarke Institute of Psychiatry and was chair of the Centered on Hope Campaign for the Center for Addiction and Mental Health Foundation. He is a founding member and a member of the committee of advisors of the Business and Economic Roundtable on Addiction and Mental Health. He and his wife,

Ana P. Lopes, are the benefactors of the Tapscott Chair in Schizophrenia Studies at the University of Toronto and were awarded the Yorktown Humanitarian Award for Community Service in 2012.

Don is an adjunct professor of management at the Joseph L. Rotman School of Management, University of Toronto. He holds a BSc in psychology and statistics, an MEd specializing in research methodology, and three doctor of laws (Hon) granted from the University of Alberta in 2001, Trent University in 2006, and McMaster University in 2010.

* * *

Patricia Titus is vice president and chief information security officer at Symantec. She is responsible for information security risk management, threat response, operational security, and governance functions. Patricia plays a strategic role in protecting Symantec's IT resources, infrastructure, and information assets, as well as driving internal security initiatives.

Prior to joining Symantec, she was vice president and global chief information security officer for Unisys Corporation, a global information technology company. At Unisys, she was responsible for enhancing the existing network security and policies supporting Unisys global employees, while ensuring the continued protection of sensitive corporate and customer data. Prior to joining Unisys, Patricia was the chief information security officer at the Transportation Security Administration within the Department of Homeland Security, where she focused on creating, implementing, and maintaining a robust IT security program.

Patricia is an active member in the Bay Area CSO Council and the Executive Women's Forum, and she serves on the Women's Advisory Board for the Girl Scouts Council of the Nation's Capital.

*   *   *

Jim Tosone is managing director, Tosone Associates. He is the creator of the Improv Means Business program, which helps organizations enhance their innovation, collaboration, and communication capabilities using the principles and techniques of applied improvisation. His clients include major corporations such as Dannon, DirecTV, MetLife, M&M Mars, Pepsi, Pfizer, and Time Warner.

He was a Pfizer Business Technology executive for 30 years; his last position was head of Pfizer Healthcare Informatics. He is a graduate of the Second City Training Center, the world's leading improvisation organization.

Jim holds BS and MS degrees from Stevens Institute of Technology.

* * *

John Yapaola is the chief executive officer at Kapow Software. He has a long, successful track record of managing and growing high-tech start-up companies. Prior to joining Kapow, John was CEO of Let's Think Wireless, a wireless infrastructure design, engineering, and installation company. Before that, he was executive vice president of business development for Paytrust (acquired by Intuit), where his responsibilities included implementing all venture and fund-raising activities.

Before Paytrust, he served as executive vice president of operations for the Americas for the Fantastic Corporation, where he built the American operation and was responsible for all sales, marketing strategies, and operations. He also served as vice president of sales at LogicWorks, then the leader in the relational database modeling and design market, where he helped lead the company to its initial public offering. He is a founding member of the New York Angels Investment Group and serves on the board of several privately held companies.

John holds a BS in business administration from Saint Peter's College.

* * *

Tony Zingale is chairman and chief executive officer of Jive Software. He is responsible for overseeing the company's overall strategic direction, planning, and execution. He currently sits on the boards of Jive Software, McAfee Software, Coverity, and Service Source.

He has nearly 30 years of experience building profitable, high-growth information technology companies. Tony most recently served as president and chief executive officer of Mercury Interactive, the worldwide leader of business technology optimization solutions. Tony successfully grew Mercury to over $1 billion in annual sales and then engineered the $5 billion merger with Hewlett-Packard that was completed at the end of 2006.

Tony holds a BS in electrical and computer engineering and a BA in business administration from the University of Cincinnati. He is a member of the University of Cincinnati Foundation's Board of Trustees.

ABOUT THE AUTHOR

Hunter Muller is president and CEO of HMG Strategy, LLC, a global IT strategy consulting firm based in Westport, Connecticut. Mr. Muller has three decades of experience in business strategy consulting. His primary focus is IT organization development, leadership, and business alignment. His concepts and programs have been used successfully by premier corporations worldwide to improve executive performance, enhance collaboration, elevate the role of IT, and align enterprise strategy across the topmost levels of management. He lives in Fairfield, Connecticut, with his wife and their two children.

ABOUT HMG STRATEGY, LLC

HMG Strategy, LLC, is a leading global provider of innovative IT leadership, management, and technology support to CIO/ senior IT executives by focusing on the 360-degree needs of the CIO/IT leader. The firm's many events and services raise thought leadership, knowledge sharing, and networking to the highest level. HMG Strategy provides access to an international network of nearly 50,000 CIO/senior IT executives, industry experts, and world-class thought leaders.

The firm's unique CIO Executive Leadership Series offers unique experiences to build relationships with peers and gain the latest insights and best practices for driving increased business value through the use of information technology. HMG Strategy events enable IT leaders to leverage the power of a worldwide network of highly talented CIOs and senior technology executives from numerous verticals and multiple sectors of the global economy.

Additionally, the firm's partnership with the world's leading executive search firms provides IT leaders with invaluable insights and opportunities for career advancement.

INDEX